I0052896

Creating Wealth by Harnessing Opportunities in Africa

God's Way to Multiply the Assets in Your Storehouses

Lauri E. Elliott
Nissi Ekpott
Hartmut Sieper

Published by Conceptualee, Inc.

Copyright © 2011 by Lauri E. Elliott, Nissi Ekpott, Hartmut Sieper

All rights reserved worldwide. No part of this book may be reproduced, stored in a retrieval system or transmitted, in any form or by any means, without the prior written consent of Conceptualee, Inc. To seek permission, send a request to info@conceptualee.com.

Published by Conceptualee, Inc.:

301 McCullough Drive, 4th Floor
Charlotte, North Carolina 28262
United States

ISBN-13 9780983301509 Print Book
ISBN-13 9780983301530 Electronic Book
06052011

Book Cover Design by Vin Furlong
Cover Background by Billy Alexander
Original Map Design (Adapted) by BSK
Antique Compass by Jamie Hansen

Business & Economics / International / General

ARISE [from the depression and prostration in which circumstances have kept you--rise to a new life]! Shine (be radiant with the glory of the Lord), for your light has come, and the glory of the Lord has risen upon you!

(Amplified Version, Isaiah 60:1)

Other titles and content on insights, resources, and strategy for business and investment in Africa can be explored at:

http://www.afribiz.info

http://www.afribiz.net

http://www.neuafrika.com

http://www.trans-africa-invest.com

http://theglobalbusinessroundtable.ning.com/

Table of Contents

Preface

Nissi Ekpott

In 2007, I watched *Africa Open for Business*[1], a BBC award-winning documentary produced by Carol Pineau from Washington, DC. It showed ten African businesses from ten countries, randomly selected, hard at work, and succeeding against many odds. It contradicted most perceptions of Africa. I got a copy and traveled with it to the United States.

I showed it to friends in Iowa. The reactions were intense and varied. The Americans watched with interest and asked many questions. Some of the Africans burst into tears of joy - at last someone was showing Africa in a new light.

Two weeks later, I was traveling from Johannesburg to Cape Town in South Africa. I had been booked to fly economy, but at the boarding gate the airline benevolently upgraded me to business class. I took my seat, tucked myself in, and then turned to say "hi" to the lady beside me. It was Carol Pineau!

I knew God had ordered our steps. We talked at length about the documentary and reasons behind it. The meeting made an impact on both of us. I got the sense that Carol saw a new future in Africa, and was working intently to show the world this future and also to be a part of it. I left knowing that things God had previously spoken to me about the African continent were unfolding.

---

[1] http://www.africaopenforbusiness.com

Since then, the global focus on Africa has grown significantly. Some believe the *Africa Open for Business* documentary played a key role, but long before this, the Lord had indicated Isaiah 60 to me as a key word for Africa. I had also met several people who had independently received the same word, in addition to other dreams, visions, and prophecies. God had shown many of His people changes - restoration, wealth, business, peace, and increase in the knowledge of Him.

Carol Pineau's documentary helped me shift from just having a prophetic expectation to applying practical, wisdom-filled, Spirit-led steps in the area of business, which would allow us to harness these expected changes.

The prayers and labor of the Church are key contributors to most of the changes we've seen already. The Western Church, over hundreds of years, has invested tremendously in Africa. And eventually, the African Church has come into a season of unprecedented growth.

We believe the Church should lead the transformation in Africa, and this can only be achieved by taking hold of the visions received in the closet, and coming out of the closet to establish them in practical ways. We believe the Church has the power and grace to touch every sphere of life across the continent, until the words come true that "… the mountain of the LORD's house shall be established in the top of the mountains, and shall be exalted above the hills; and all nations shall flow unto it." (King James Version, Isaiah 2:2). [2]

This book is designed to help readers achieve the shift from prophetic expectation to practical, Spirit-led application. Our desire is to stir up, and see practically involved, believers in the body of

---

[2] Unless otherwise noted, the remaining quotes from scripture in this book come from the King James Version.

Christ - those who've already received conviction about Africa's restoration and its role in the future. For those who've had no inkling of God's plans for the continent and hear us, we encourage you to go to God in prayer and receive guidance.

This book primarily targets Christian business people. But, we believe everyone should read it.

We hope that as a person of God, who is reading through these pages, you will share our belief in the continent and take practical steps to partake in the wealth, in all its facets, that this continent holds.

Also, we hope the Church will be able to shift from a focus only on aid to Africa, to a place of investing in viable business ventures, which is the only way to release wealth.

And, we hope that as Christians invest and contribute to change in Africa, they too will find God's transforming power to change their lives, grow their faith, and make them more like Him. Through our collective investment, Africa will be prepared to play its God-given role as a place of refuge, abundant provision, healing, wisdom, and restoration to a hurting world.

Our sincere thanks to all those whose support has made this book a possibility. We are not able to mention all your names, but as you read this, you'll know who you are because you have invested directly, or indirectly, in the lives of the authors and producers of this book. True success is usually a collective effort. May God water your life abundantly.

And finally, thanks and praise to our Lord and King, Jesus, for without Him nothing is possible and in Him all things are possible.

Nissi Ekpott
January 11, 2011

Foreword

Sipho Mseleku

President, Pan African Chambers of Commerce and Industry

Creating Wealth by Harnessing Opportunities in Africa is one of the few excellently written and well-researched books on exploring business, trade, and investment opportunities on the African continent. It is unique in that it focuses on the Christian community.

It delves deeply into Africa's present, future, and the "kairos" moment for Africa to take its place as a leading citizen of the world, spiritually, socially, and economically. As *Creating Wealth* points out, Africa's vast economic, as well as trade and investment, opportunities remain mostly unexplored.

The book is also anchored on sound biblical and spiritual principles and values while carefully exposing Africa's magnificent economic potential among the nations of the world. The book makes us understand God's plan for Africa's restoration and its pre-eminent place in the future political, as well as socioeconomic, global landscape.

Africa is a large continent, has vast natural, mineral, agricultural, forestry, water, and energy resources, and a growing consumer market. This presents great opportunities for business and economic development, which will result in Africa being able to exert political influence globally.

This book will be a powerful guide for Christians and global businesses intending to invest and expand into Africa. The book is also a powerful tool in the hands of African businesses to realize what God has bestowed in Africa and how they can tap into the opportunities presented by Africa for the betterment of all.

We, at the Global Business Roundtable, are privileged to be associated and working with the authors – Lauri, Nissi, and Hartmut.

Sipho Mseleku
President, Global Business Roundtable
Chairman, Global Fund for Christ
President, Pan African Chambers of Commerce and Industry

About the Global Business Roundtable

The Global Business Roundtable is a platform and network for business people from various backgrounds and religions to come together to network and exchange ideas on business, career, and professional development. Its primary focus is on complete development of a person, including business development, skills development, wealth creation, estate planning, networking, mentorship, business and procurement opportunities, as well as spiritual development.

http://theglobalbusinessroundtable.ning.com/

About the Global Fund for Christ

The Global Fund for Christ (GFC) is a fund established in line with a mandate given by the Holy Spirit in 2007. It focuses on the upliftment of poor people in developing communities in underdeveloped regions around the world. GFC develops assets for education (e.g., building schools, providing educational training and infrastructure). It will also focus on health care, poverty alleviation, food security, and job creation projects.

http://www.globalfundforchrist.com

Pan African Chambers of Commerce and Industry

The Pan African Chambers of Commerce and Industry (PACCI) is a continental chamber, representing 53 African countries. It is the single largest business body on the African continent. Its role is summed up in this phrase, "The voice of business in Africa".

1

Introduction:
"Africa Rising" Prophecies
Hartmut Sieper
Lauri Elliott

We (Hartmut, Nissi, and Lauri) want to welcome you to the journey to explore and engage with Africa. It's an amazing place filled with amazing people and potential.

The road for Africa, and those associated with it, has not typically been an easy one. It has been paved with pain and danger, disappointment, upheaval, and conflict for many. But the misery of yesteryear has started to turn into magnificence. I (Lauri) love the passages, "…weeping may endure for the night, but joy comes in the morning." (Psalm 30:4) and "He hath made all things beautiful in his time." (Ecclesiastes 3:11).

We look forward to sharing this time of joy and beauty for Africa with you.

Streams of Prophecies about Africa

Hartmut's Introduction to Africa
I still remember the day when the Lord drew me (Hartmut) to Africa for the first time. It was in a very difficult season of my life; when I fervently prayed to the Lord and asked Him to show me His divine purpose for my life.

In a cell group of my home church in Frankfurt, Germany, I suddenly had a subtle thought as the Lord whispered to me, "What would you say if I sent you to Africa?" I was very surprised, because as an investment professional I did not have any connection to Africa. And, I was convinced that the negative headlines of the mainstream media were true. Nothing could be further from my personal situation and occupational perspectives than Africa. I also didn't know any African at the time. So, I forgot about that.

Two years after that incident, I realized that the commodity markets had entered into a new secular bull (positive, growing) trend. (Secular trends last for decades.) Africa as a resource-rich continent came to mind.

When I was sitting before my globe on one rainy afternoon, I recognized Africa as the last white spot on the investment landscape of the world. I had the gut feeling that global emerging markets investors would ultimately shift focus to Africa. It should be the right time for bold entrepreneurs and investors with foresight to invest in countries like Angola, where a long civil war had almost entirely destroyed the country's infrastructure. Doing so, follows the advice of Baron Rothschild to buy when there is "blood in the streets."

At the same time, the Lord started to instruct me about the future of the world financial systems in general and the key role of gold in particular. In 2004, I decided to write a book about the future collapse of the financial system and how to best prepare for that inevitable development. For many months, I worked on the table of contents and tried to combine both the secular world and the prophetic perspective. I couldn't get a clue, so I thought the plan wasn't from the Lord.

My kairos moment as an author came later. In 2007, I got the idea for another book, about investing in Africa. This time, writing the table of contents for a book of 500 pages took me only four hours.

A few weeks later, I arranged a meeting with the publisher of the most renowned publishing company of financial books in Germany. I presented my book concept to him, and after 15 minutes he agreed to publish the book and to cover all costs that would be involved.

So, I felt the favor of the Lord on me. It took me four months to do the necessary research and to write the book. It was the first book about investments in Africa on the German-speaking book market and it opened many doors.

In 2005, I followed the advice of the Lord not to buy any stocks. That was a huge challenge for me, because dealing with stocks had been my profession for more than 20 years. Instead, I started buying physical gold. In those times, God spoke to other people as well about accumulating wealth in gold. Looking back from now to that decision to shift from stocks into gold, I am very grateful to the Lord since gold was one of the very few asset classes that had not been negatively affected by the world financial crisis from 2007 to 2009. As a matter of fact, the precious metal's price more than doubled.

Two years later, I joined the International Christian Chamber of Commerce, ICCC, and attended the annual general meeting in Altensteig, Germany in 2006. At that time, I learned that God is the God of the last minute. Just four days before the conference actually started, the Lord downloaded the business concept of Trans Africa Invest to me. It was an overwhelming experience, as I saw many puzzle pieces moving together into a powerful picture.

I quickly prepared a presentation of the basic business concept, and shared my vision about bringing investors from Germany to African markets to the African delegation at the conference. Within the next three days, I met some wonderful business people from various African countries, who are now working closely with me. In 2007, I made my first long reconnaissance trip through Africa and founded the company of Trans Africa Invest in Germany, as well as our first affiliate company in Zambia.

As I was a very new member of ICCC, I didn't know about the special role of Africa within the organization. I learned that some profound prophecies on Africa turning into a new season had already been given, and that bringing business and investments into the continent of Africa could well be a fulfillment of these prophecies.

Africa in the Global Marketplace

Indeed, over the last 10 years some prophecies suggested that Africa would play a vital role in the global marketplace. Humble believers from all over the world got revelations from the Lord, which stand in stark contrast to the average perception of Africa as the forgotten continent full of poverty, crime, diseases, civil wars, and widespread underdevelopment.

Let's take a look into some of those prophecies and learn about God's picture of Africa and His plans for the continent. It is breathtaking and mind blowing. It is the opposite of what the world thinks about Africa. Be prepared for some radical paradigm shifts, which will be outlined in subsequence chapters of this book.

Gunnar Olson, the founder of ICCC, prophesied in Johannesburg in 2000 that Africa will arise:

> *Africa - this is your kairos moment; therefore arise, and take your destiny.*
>
> *Africa - be released and accept your divine mandate from heaven.*
>
> *Africa - your shackles of slavery, poverty, limitations, idolatry, paganism, discrimination, exploitation, servitude, perversion, discord, ancestor worship, Satanism, and all evil is crushed.*

Arise! Arise! Arise!

Africa - bring forth your sons and daughters who will arise and take their rightful place among kings, princes, and nobles of the earth. Let them execute the righteousness of God, and advance the purposes of God to bring healing, prosperity, and manifestations of majesty, excellence, and glory.

Africa - the Lord will build a highway of holiness and righteousness, and everyone who walks on this highway will find refuge, strength, and purpose.

Africa - all the nations of the earth will come to marvel at your wisdom and glory.

Africa, oh Africa - the deepest fountains and resources of heaven that have been hidden in your belly because of the deeds of evil men, are now breaking forth because of the remnant that has regarded the will of God higher than the opinions of men.

Africa - Arise! Arise! Arise! For God has risen upon you and your enemies are scattered.

When these words were spoken, something happened in the spiritual realm. In his prophecy that was given on his visit to Ndola, Zambia in July 2002, the Afrikaner prophet, Andre Koetzee said:[3]

...I saw in a picture God blowing on the ground of Ndola and Zambia. As He did, dust and sand were blowing away. An old foundation was laid bare. These are ancient plans God has had since the beginning of time for this place. He's revealing and bringing them to the fore once again.

---

[3] Edited by Pr. Derek Mutungu for Zambia Intercessory Network and ICCC Zambia.

And I saw the airport, with big new hangars being built. There were lots of airplanes - big and small - flying into Ndola. Hundreds of people kept coming off those planes. They are God's children, sent by Him. They stay in your homes. You house, feed, encourage, and support them. Then, you send them in groups on planes to different countries all over Africa. You send them to different countries and to unreached places.

I felt the Lord say, "My purpose for you is to reach Africa. You will be a landing strip, a place of launching ministries from the South of Africa to the rest of Africa."

And the Lord says, "Don't worry about resources. Your riches and supplies will not come from America or other countries anymore. They will come out of THIS ground, out of THIS place. For I will reveal resources you never knew you had."

So prepare yourselves, your households, your lives. Some of you will be leaders among these groups.

The Lord says, "He has saved Africa for last." He says, "Africa is my precious jewel I've saved for last. And Africa is coming to the forefront. The jewel of Africa - its people - will be revealed."

He's lifting Africa up above all other continents in the world. He'll do a thing here never seen anywhere else. People will stream from ALL OVER to Africa to see what the Lord has done. They will come to find God, to find revival, to find fire, to find redemption in Africa.

"The Lord has saved Africa for last." Wow, what a thought! I remember that the Lord told me something similar, when some Christians talked to me that the very last days of the end times have begun, and that Jesus Christ would return very shortly. From my perspective, we cannot know the day or hour of His return. Jesus states that very clearly in Matthew 25:13, "Therefore keep watch, because you do not know the day or the hour." (New International Version).

There is another reason why one should be careful to predict a soon return of Jesus. How could our Savior return at a time when He had already blessed all nations and regions of the earth at one time or another, except for Africa? Could he forget Africa? To be honest, I cannot believe that. It is somewhat logical to assume that the Lord finally would bless Africa abundantly, before the second coming of Jesus.

Another biblical verse popped into my mind, "But many who are first will be last, and many who are last will be first." (New International Version, Matthew 19:30). Can it be true that Africa, the forgotten continent, will be placed before all other regions of the world? Africans have suffered so much in the last centuries.

The former president of Zambia, Frederick Chiluba, received the following Word from the Lord on June 30, 1999, and spoke it out in the State House during negotiations for the peace of the Democratic Republic of Congo (DRC):

> *My People Will Rise Again*
> *The door is wide open to you my people.*
> *For long for so long for ever so long, you have languished under a heavy yoke of suffering, pain, and agony.*
> *You have been oppressed. Despised as the scum of the earth, treated by all as nothings.*
> *You (have) gone about your narrow pathways with your heads bowed low.*
> *But a new day has dawned when my people will rise again.*

For I am pouring my glory in a fresh new way upon the people of this continent. I am raising a horn of salvation for them. I will make all of you glorious in my sight and (others).

For you have turned your heart towards me, you have forsaken the ways of your forefathers. You have inclined your ears towards me. For this reason, I am raising this people to new levels of glory, honor, and power. I am obliterating your shame.

How Zambia, as a nation, was born is an interesting story. When David Livingstone, the famous traveler who was also a *missionary and philanthropist,* "discovered" this region for the Western world, he fell in love with the country. Before he died in 1873 at Bangweulu Lake in today's Zambia, he dedicated this place to God. Following his commitment, "My heart is in Africa", his heart was taken out of his corpse and buried in African soil. When Zambia gained independence in 1964, the nation was founded as a Christian nation.

Beyond all worldly thoughts and economic considerations about the future of Africa, we as the body of Christ must also take spiritual revelations into account. Africans, as well as African Americans, much better understand the reality of the spiritual realm than white people normally do. So, Africans should build on this God-given strength rather than following the worldly view of neglecting or minimizing it.

Allowing the Holy Spirit to guide oneself through business life and all issues that have to do with money is a wise decision and foresighted approach. Being guided by the Holy Spirit includes trying to see Africa from a godly perspective. This perspective is very different from what the world thinks about Africa. A good way to start with the new perspective is to consciously recall the paradigm shifts and new mindsets we will share in the following chapters.

Transfer of Wealth

Many things have been said about the transfer of wealth from the world into the Kingdom of God. Christians from all over the world have been looking forward to seeing this happen in reality for many years. However, things were moving more slowly than expected by most believers, creating disappointment and discouragement. At a prophetic conference in Colorado Springs in 2004 that I attended, Peter C. Wagner made an interesting statement when he talked about transfer of wealth: there must be enough humble servants in place in key positions of the marketplace, before this long anticipated process actually can start and be sustained.

The following remarkable prophetic words over business in South Africa were received by Derick Botha, Chairman, ICCC South Africa, Agriculture Domain, on August 6, 2006:

It is important not to be tied up in a Western way of thinking where the only alternative to capitalism is seen as socialism. Neither of these systems will work in Africa. There is a new way of working and functioning that the Lord wants us to discover for Africa, but He first wants us to stop filtering everything through our westernized paradigms of good vs. bad and profit vs. loss. This is not the way God wants to work in Africa because the moment you start investing into society and community - laying down your business to invest into people lives - there is profit.

This economic era is drawing to the close and there is a new reality coming in which accountancy-based thinking of profit and loss will be replaced with a new thing God is doing.

One of the hidden values in African culture is the value of communication, shared meaning, and connecting. This represents a new way of functioning because it is not about the bottom line; it's about people, connecting, and having a relationship.

The Lord has a new way of thinking and, if we go into Africa with the idea of saving the "Dark Continent" with our wonderful ideas, we are going to miss it because it's a mutual thing that is happening. As the Lord sends us to Africa, He is actually sending Africa to us to bring a change in the way we think and the way we function and the way we do things. God is going to take us into a brotherhood and partnership and a new way of functioning.

Africa will receive a new philosophy of business, social structures, development, wealth, and quality of life. This new philosophy will confound science and technology and the Western and Eastern paradigms. The Lord will raise the African academics up with a new way of incorporating what He is into the way people think and do.

Surely, it is not easy for Westerners to lay aside the way of thinking that we are accustomed to. It is a challenge to look at Africa in a new way. In order to do something new in and with Africa in the realm of business and investment, being guided by the Holy Spirit, you have to leave the beaten track. By moving out of your comfort zone, you might be thrown into a truly adventurous environment. Brave men and women, be honest with yourself. Isn't this something that you have a desire for deep in your heart?

Derick Botha continued:

A new principle and standard will come forth in Africa saying that firstly the African people must benefit before any company is allowed to benefit. New laws and legislation may be put in place that will enforce this. We will not see any more that most of the riches leave Africa to benefit the other countries of the world before it benefits Africa.

The riches God has placed in African people all over the world, where they are in the diaspora, will be returned to Africa. He is bringing back Africa's children from all over the world where they were sent to be strengthened. Many of them are frustrated. They long for Africa, but fear that due to the poverty and corruption in Africa, there is no space for them to function in their callings. The Lord is cutting off this lie.

...

Even within Africa, the Lord is sending exiled children home to their nations with the riches they have gathered. They will come back slowly, but surely. Financial disasters in the West are about to destroy the things the exiles build their lives on. The exiles will return with the riches of the world in their heads. The Lord will bring them back to Africa and establish systems through the knowledge they have. They will have integrity.

The Lord is coming against the shame in the African people that have left, and giving them godly pride for their nations. The Lord will bring them back with pride and delight, with gifts and callings, ministries, and skills. With pride, they will begin to build. The Lord says Africa is something, Africa is important to God. His focus and attention is on Africa and on the children of Africa.

Children of Africa

I strongly believe that Africans in the diaspora will play a vital role in restoring and developing sound businesses in their home countries in Africa. They will bring home not only new ideas and the knowledge of the developed world, but also capital and the ability to change things in Africa. As they know both worlds, the Western environment of their host countries as well as the traditional thinking in their home countries, they are predestined to function as connecting links and gateways.

Chad Taylor, who prophesied on Africa at Victory Christian Fellowship, Fresno, California in February 17, 2008, also mentioned the children of Africa returning home:

> *Africa - mighty nation of kings and princes - the Lord says to Africa, Rachel, weep no more. Your children are coming back to their borders and every anointing that was forfeited, sold, and stolen on every foreign sea shore will return to your continent a hundred fold in this lifetime, in this lifetime and the life to come. For I see Esau coming back to Jacob; I see the army of Esau and all his lambs and sheep; I see the wealth of Esau coming back to Jacob; I see the Queen of Sheba coming unto Solomon.*
>
> *I see the wealth of the wicked returning, returning to the shores of Africa and you will rebuild the old waste places and the cities that have been ashes God will raise up before your eyes, even like a new Jerusalem. God will raise up a city, God will raise up a continent, and God will raise up a nation even in a day.*
>
> *...*
>
> *Great charity will break poverty and Africa will become a storehouse to the nations. Storehouses filled with new manna and new bread and other countries in the next decade will come to Africa to fill their bags and fill their ships. I will completely turn it around for all things work together for the good for those called according to My purposes and my purposes are coming into fullness, fullness.*

Africa - Storehouse of the World
In line with many other prophets, Chad Taylor mentioned that Africa
will become a storehouse for the world. This element can be found in
many prophecies on Africa. From a business point of view, this can
really happen. From a prophetic point of view, it will happen. And
from a global point of view of a sustainable world, it must happen.
Within the next 20 years, 2 billion more people will be on the planet
Earth and have to be fed.

The world food systems use just-in-time methodology, meaning
food resources cover less than three months of the world's demand.
There are huge challenges awaiting us. We simply do not grow
enough food for all people. Growing energy crops will increase the
food shortage even further.

The good news is that there is still plenty of land that can be
cultivated. Africa is the continent with the highest productivity
reserves in the world. 60% of the unused arable land worldwide can
be found in Africa, according to the McKinsey Global Institute.[4]
Tremendous opportunities in farming, ranching, and food processing
are waiting for bold entrepreneurs. By making unproductive land
productive, the value of the land can be increased easily, instantly
leading to a higher company value.

The following prophecy was given at Kaniki Bible College,
Zambia, on January 30, 2004:

*I surely want to turn this land into a bread basket. People
far and wide will see what I do through you and for you and
marvel at my ways. I will gain fame through you, great*

---

[4] McKinsey Global Institute. (2010). Lions on the Move: The Progress and Potential
of African Economies (Executive Summary). Accessed online at
http://www.mckinsey.com/mgi/publications/progress_and_potential_of_african_ec
onomies/pdfs/MGI_african_economies_ExecSumm.pdf (January 8, 2011).

renown in the entire land of Havilah. I am releasing great riches. My storehouse is open. My bounty is freely let loose. I am pouring it out upon the land.

According to scientists, the country of Zambia alone with 12 million people living in an area of the size of Texas, could easily feed more than 100 million people if the land is cultivated with Western methods. However, agriculture and agribusiness are very capital intensive. To unlock the agricultural resources of big African countries like Angola, Mozambique, Zambia, Zimbabwe, and both Congos, massive investments have to be made. As so often, big challenges are connected with big opportunities.

Prophecies on Specific Countries

Dr. Chuck Pierce prophesied in Lusaka, Zambia in 2008 on Zimbabwe:

> *I'm here to announce to you that because of this meeting tonight and because of the border between Zambia and Zimbabwe, in eighteen months God will have turned that nation upside down. And I'm here to tell you, eighteen months from today, watch how God starts developing a strategy and a structure to turn that nation upside down. Look out for how He will begin to rearrange it, for the glory of God will sweep from this boundary into Zimbabwe.*

Shortly after that prophecy, Zimbabwe turned upside down in reality. A new government of unity had been formed, bringing President Robert Mugabe and the leader of the opposing party, Morgan Tsvangirai, as prime minister, to share power in this nation. The hyperinflationary currency of Zimbabwe, the Zimbabwe Dollar, had been abandoned in March 2009, giving way to a multi-currency regime with the U.S. Dollar and South African Rand, as commonly used legal tender. Since then, inflation is under control, and the economy quickly regained momentum.

While the Western world is on a downward path in financial, economic, and spiritual terms, Africa is on the rise. Interaction between the Western world and Africa is about to change radically. This might lead much further than most people would expect.

A positive and surprising outlook was given to Catherine Brown on January 20, 2010, when she had a powerful dream: [5]

> *I saw again the continent of Africa, and understood I was looking down through many centuries of time into the past. I witnessed nations come from the West to enslave Africans and my heart was broken.*
>
> *Then an amazing thing happened in my dream as we transitioned to present-time revelation: The "tables were turned" and the one who had formerly been enslaved was now no longer a slave; and this African person reached out in mercy to the one from the West who had made them a slave, and immediately bridges of mercy appeared all over Africa.*
>
> *The release of mercy caused Africa's borders to extend as bridges of God's mercy, sent to reach the nations. The bridges speak of African Believers anointed with the mercy of God to bring restoration to those who are now enslaved to sin in the West. Africa grew in size in my dream as God's mercy was extended - this speaks of the advancement of God's Kingdom on earth through the ministry of African servants of the Lord.*

---

[5]Brown, C. (February 23, 2010). The Dream: Africa Ablaze with God's Glory. Accessed online at http://www.elijahlist.com/words/display_word.html?ID=8512 (January 7, 2011).

God spoke to me by His Spirit and said, "The Enslaved shall become the Emancipator." Under the anointing described in Isaiah 61, African Believers are being sent out to the nations to bring deliverance to Western nations who are now entrenched (and thus enslaved) in sin.

It is my firm belief that this is God's kairos time for the West to receive Africa's anointed, end-time leaders as they are commissioned to serve God's purposes and plans in the nations. As I shared the dream and its interpretation, I prophesied that Africa had entered her sovereign timeline for revival and would experience an exodus of redemption.

It is my sincere conviction that Africa is a gateway continent, which means that whatever is bound and loosed in Africa, will therefore be bound and loosed on the earth. Through Africa, the West can receive blessing or cursing, depending on who is doing the binding and the loosing!

If the Church in Africa will rise up and take her place in divine destiny, God is going to release mighty waves of His redemptive glory through African ministers and ministries that will bring transformation to the nations.

God not only speaks through dreams and prophetic words, but He also demonstrates his presence through manifestations and natural signs. A big white cross appeared in the blue sky in Kenya after a conference on doing agriculture God's way in Nairobi in 2007.

This cross appeared at Naivasha, on the Nairobi-Nakuru Highway in the Kenyan Rift Valley. (Photo by: Okotch Mondoh)

Some of the participants made a trip through the Rift Valley in central Kenya. When they prayed, they saw the cross. The same incident happened some years ago, when some members of the same group gathered in a prayer meeting in Moolmanshoek, South Africa.

Africa, America, and a New Economic System

Lauri's Introduction to Africa

My (Lauri's) experience is like that of Hartmut. Africa was never on my radar as a destination, even though I am African American. My academic studies included history and political science focused on Western Europe, including the Western Mediterranean. I found that I loved studying this sphere.

About eight years ago, I decided to take a shift in my life and move to southern Europe on the Mediterranean – Spain, Italy, or France. At this same time, I started to take a deeper dive into the Bible, including the historical context and stories behind God's Word. I began to see the lack of understanding I had about the Eastern Mediterranean, including Israel, so I thought that I would travel to Haifa to study for a period of time.

This life had no purpose to it, so God interceded. At the time, a friend in the military was stationed in Egypt and I thought this would be as good of a place as any to start my new life. I even made connection with a Christian organization, which provides education for thousands of children in Egypt to help them develop curriculum, as my profession was instructional design and organizational development.

This never happened because I got cold feet at the time. I didn't see how I would have enough to support myself. I had expected to work on projects remotely, but nothing transpired. So, even though I had a ticket, I chickened out.

This was in the spring of 2004. I remember the agony I felt for the next month. I cried out to God. I was ashamed that I had chickened out. But during this time, another colleague began to share his experience with South Africa and plans to move there later in the year.

It was then that I began to do more research about Africa and learned of the plight of Africa amidst the riches found there. Being a systems-oriented person, my thought was that the poverty there was a man-made problem, which is true. Centuries of colonialism, imperialism, slavery, and oppression are the roots of the poverty in Africa today.

So, I moved to South Africa in February 2005 on a leap of faith. That leap of faith took me from prosperity to poverty. I learned what it was to be without a home, not have enough food to eat, and to be an outcast. I learned what it was like to have people try to use you as a slave for your skills and intellect.

But I also learned that I had a lot that had to be changed within me. I could not go as a Western "savior" to a land given to others and dictate how things could be done. I couldn't believe that God intended that any human being dominate others. There were other things about my character that needed a lot of work.

I had a lot to learn and it wasn't a pretty road. It's not a road I would wish on my worst enemy in fact. But even in this dark time, I found wonderful, supportive, and helpful Christian brothers and sisters in South Africa.

Through it all, God gave me clear revelation about Africa's place in the world from an economic perspective, as well as strategies and practical insights to catalyze it. In the following section, I share the prophetic revelation God has given. And, we (Nissi, Hartmut, and Lauri) share the strategies and practical insights God has given us, as well as knowledge He has allowed to come our way, in the rest of the book.

Experiencing the Kingdom of Heaven on Earth: Africa - A Start for a New Economic System (2006-2008)

Africa is one of God's hidden treasures that will be leveraged to bring economic justice to the world. Africa is a key epicenter for the "new" Kingdom-based economic system, which God is strategically establishing to bless not only the "true" Church but the nations. Africa possesses a significant purpose and position in God's vision for the last age.

I want to share what I understand of God's vision for Africa and how He is manifesting it at this time. But more so, I want to tap into your spirit and witness your mind transform, so that you see with your heart how God is calling you to work with and for Africa to bless the world. This talk, this sharing, speaks of both the prophetic and the practical.

The Bible says that God does nothing without first telling His prophets. It also says that the men of Issachar understood the times (1 Chronicles 12:32). The hand of God we see working in current events has been declared beforehand. He also wants us – His people – to understand what He is doing. I would like to share some of what I understand concerning Africa and its impact on the world economy.

I will weave these revelations together for you through the lens God has given me as an African American living out her purpose in Africa. Let me share a little of my heritage. I was born during the Civil Rights Era in the 1960s in Michigan in the United States. My parents were still living out racial/social injustice, even though we lived in the Midwest in the United States. As their child, I received all the benefits from struggles and victories of the Civil Rights movement and my parents. I was brought up in a nuclear family with parents that supported and loved me, gave me an excellent education, and open doors of opportunity that they never had. God blessed me with a wonderful family and life. I would never trade the childhood God gave me. My question to myself was, "if I experienced the fruits of the Civil Rights era, what am I to do in this generation and leave for the next?"

This year (2008) marks the 40th anniversary of Martin Luther King's death – the passing of another generation. So, what is God doing in this generation? It would seem that since Martin Luther King there has been "a wilderness" concerning justice for all people. What could God be asking this generation to do? I am totally convicted that God is calling those born during the Civil Rights Era, American or otherwise, to pursue a new movement for justice to touch people everywhere.

Psalm 82:2-5 (Amplified Version) says:

2How long will you [magistrates or judges] judge unjustly and show partiality to the wicked? Selah [pause, and calmly think of that]!

3Do justice to the weak (poor) and fatherless; maintain the rights of the afflicted and needy.

4Deliver the poor and needy; rescue them out of the hand of the wicked.

5[The magistrates and judges] know not, neither will they understand; they walk on in the darkness [of complacent satisfaction]; all the foundations of the earth [the fundamental principles upon which rests the administration of justice] are shaking.

But our mission is not the same as the past generation. They fought for racial and social justice; we are to fight for economic justice. This is a key movement in the next wave of God's hand, or direct intervention, in the affairs of men. As the foundations of the earth were shaken by racial and social justice movements then, they will be shaken again and are being done so now over economic justice.

Once you begin to grasp this revelation, it is important that you understand what justice means. Justice simply means setting things right. Today, economic injustice is mostly characterized by economic inequity – the rich getting richer and the poor getting poorer in a systematic, deliberate way.

I believe that Martin Luther King had a glimpse of God's vision concerning economic justice and began the work that his death put to a stop. When he was killed, King was headed for Washington, DC to do a similar rally for the poor that was done for civil rights. The irony is the place he was killed – Memphis – was an unscheduled stop.

While he was starting in the United States, it seems his heart was to bring relief to the poor everywhere. We now have a call and opportunity to carry this forward like Joshua did in the place of Moses when he caused the children of Israel to take possession of their Promised Land (Joshua 1:6; Joshua 23:14).

God has shown a key to unlocking and releasing economic justice. Satan is using distraction so that we expend most of energy trying to tame the existing world economic and financial system. We spend so much time, effort, resources, and money to this end. God says He is creating a new thing (Isaiah 43:10) – a new economic system.

This new economic system can be designed to benefit all and realize the Kingdom of Heaven manifested on earth. This is much more productive than chasing a system that is now showing the rottenness of its roots and is imploding itself. This past year has been light for all of us, but perhaps painful for many with the economic and financial crises, particularly in the United States.

We can create a new economic system, starting small but built for sustainability and rapid growth. As it grows, it will overpower the existing world systems. In addition, as the world system continues to roll back its control over territory, God's ordained economic system naturally takes possession of those territories.

We can see this principle in God's creation – vast, dense forests. The forests started as individual trees that started as seeds which grew into mature trees which were able to reproduce. In fact, the Edenic and Abrahamic covenants reveal this process – be fruitful, multiply, replenish, and take dominion.

Again, I need to take a side line to clarify the concept of dominion. The word "dominion" causes some to bristle and others to shout "hallelujah." Myles Munroe explains what dominion means so well. Freedom, or "free to dominate," according to God's Kingdom is free to dominate the unique space or purpose God has given to you on this earth in His service and that of people. Freedom, or free to dominate, does not mean controlling or dominating people.

In fact, when we do this it becomes sin. In fact, the world system illustrates this. Through its perversion, it is designed to control and dominate people, placing them in bondage and oppression. We can certainly see this in our political, economic, and financial systems.

In essence, this "new" economic system is an instrument to serve God and people. It serves as a tangible vehicle for seeing the Kingdom of God in action on the earth while blessing the people of the earth. The Lord is using and blessing Kingdom-minded people like you and me, as well as Kingdom-driven organisms like the African New Economy Workgroup (see Appendix A).

I pray at this point that what I have said connected with your spirit and you see one of the "what's" of God's vision for this time. Now that we understand some of the "what" and "when", we need to explore how God is choosing to do this. This is where Africa comes in the picture as a key instrument in this "new" economic system.

I came to Africa – South Africa – in 2005 with an understanding that God was going to use Africa as a key seat of power to demonstrate his Kingdom on earth. He essentially sent me ahead to position me for my purpose as well. He showed a vision of prosperity for Africa – one which was recently born.

Imagine the tree King Nebuchadnezzar saw in a dream, which represented His Kingdom (Daniel 4:10-12). Like this tree, the "African" kingdom has "food for all in it" and "all flesh is fed from it".

My first specific re-collection of this vision came when the words "Africa will save America" came to my spirit and I began to speak it to others. Of course, this sounded ridiculous to most at the time, particularly when speaking financially. However, in the current environment, it no longer seems so ridiculous or impossible.

I believe that God has allowed the massive potential of Africa to benefit the world and do good to be hidden for this appointed time. The United States and the West (the Church included) have pumped trillions of dollars in development, aid, etc. into Africa in the past century, which seems to have yielded little significant impact economically.

This has fed an image of Africa as a child that needs to be taken care of and one perhaps that will never stand on its own. In fact, Africa is known as the "Dark Continent." When you check satellite images of the earth at night, showing the illumination of lights, Africa literally sits in virtual darkness.

But, our God is amazing. God kept one of his most precious jewels for a time when it would make the most significant impact.

While there is no escaping the world financial crisis in the developed world, particularly in the West, the extent to which the crisis hits Africa has a lot to do with how Africa responds to the crisis. The World Bank says that even in a period of recession for the West, the average Gross Domestic Product (GDP) in Sub-Saharan African countries should remain around 6% over the next year. (Sub-Saharan Africa actually maintained a GDP between 4% and slightly over 5% between 2008 and 2010.)

Large Western firms and investors are still sending people to investigate and take over major economic opportunities in Africa. The question is are we going to just stand by and let this happen when we can use the same African potential to create economic justice for everyone?

It's important to understand what I call the "Africa Rising" revelation, which you can see from Gunnar Olson's prophecy, many others, and what was revealed to me, is beyond any one person or organization.

The biblical text passage, which is the basis of this revelation, is Isaiah 60:1-5. First, this passage speaks of a time when strong darkness covers the earth. We are in one of those periods now. The world financial, economic, and market systems are imploding.

There is a restlessness or dissatisfaction among massive numbers of people in how their countries and lives have been governed. (One recent example is the mass protests in Tunisia, which led to President Zine el-Abidine Ben Ali stepping down after over 20 years. Some believe this will lead to a wave of Arab governmental shifts.)

Second, this passage speaks of God shining light, or glory, during this time upon Jerusalem. Jerusalem means place of peace. The Hebrew word for peace is shalom, which does not mean a cessation of conflict but completeness – nothing missing. As Africa grows strong and pre-eminent during this time, it will not be just about economics and social concerns, but first spiritual.

This is a part of the revival we have been waiting for. This is an opportunity to see the Kingdom of God come to earth first through the spirit of men, then through the minds of men with the mind of Christ and finally in a physical, self-sustaining system designed to bless all people like the Garden of Eden.

Third, the passage speaks of the glory of Jerusalem drawing everyone to it - drawing sons and daughters (Africans by heart and those in the diaspora) and Gentiles (those not considered part of the household) who want to be part of the blessing. If we look at our spiritual family, it represents the millions of Christians everywhere.

Fourth, the passage speaks of the wealth that will be brought to Jerusalem by these people, who are gathering together. In the context of Africa, it is people and organizations bringing their treasures – money, resources, talents, ideas, innovations, and strengths - to

Africa to bless it. In doing so, Africa becomes a blessing to the rest of the world.

This is where we begin to see how Africa fits into God's paradigm of a new economic system. As blessings are released to create an economic system, blessings are released through the system to people in Africa and around the world.

Structures Developed to Follow Prophecy

I used to head a company called Shujaa Intermediary Network Consortium (SINC) in South Africa, which is now a division of my company, Conceptualee, Inc. in the United States. The SINC division's mission fits well with God's purpose for Africa:

> *To bring people and resources, inside and outside Africa, to create, nurture, and grow a sustainable continental ecosystem, which is inclusive of all who live on the African continent economically and socially. This is accomplished through implementing for-profit ventures and economic systems that are linked together, work synergistically and synchronously across the continent, and place people as the foci.*

This has moved to another level by the establishment of ANEW, which has the sole purpose of catalyzing such an economic system. While it is an innovation of God, it is designed to include anyone who connects with the vision – both Christian and Non-Christian.

A lot more can be said of what this "new" economic system is, what it will do, and the outcomes, but this talk is just to share the vision and find out if you are one of those who will bring your wealth – all that you are (spirit, mind, and body) to bless Africa so Africa can bless others.

And finally, in the midst of the global financial crisis while the West was struggling, Africa did arise and its position in the world started to become more visible. We will explore this in more detail in the next chapter.

Conclusion

We (Nissi, Hartmut, and Lauri) recognize that what we have said and will say in the remaining chapters is a lot to process at one time, but whatever strikes a chord with you meditate on that and seek the Lord's revelation.

What we do understand is that God has many more servants like us in place to see and work with the "Africa Rising" anointing, or mantle, if we can call it as such. It is an anointing that will touch the entire world and bring hope, healing, and prosperity to the broad society, or nations.

As a reader of this book, you may have a role to play, however small or great. Ask yourself and the Lord about your destiny, the divine task that the Lord assigned to you, and Africa's place in them. From a practical side, there are many things that you can do, such as:

- Embrace the vision of Africa as a promising investment destination and a business hub with a bright future.
- Gather and share information.
- Make your knowledge and experience available to Africa and Africans.
- Start a business, or invest, in Africa. Establish new trade routes to or from Africa.
- Tell your boss that there are good opportunities in Africa.
- Connect people.
- Write an article.

We look forward to meeting, connecting, and working with you on this journey.

2

The New Africa:
An Emerging Manifestation

Hartmut Sieper

Lauri Elliott

Nissi Ekpott

This chapter reflects the fast changing paradigm called Africa. The first decade in the 21st century saw Africa push forth on the international scene as a place of light instead of darkness. Many of you will be amazed.

Economic Transformation on the Continent

While private wealth in developed nations struggles to recover from the economic crisis, the situation in Africa is remarkably bright. Africa, the colorful continent that consists of 53 nations (soon to be 54 nations with the secession of Southern Sudan from Northern Sudan) has prepared the stage for abundant wealth creation in this decade and beyond.

Major paradigm shifts can be observed in the world that will dramatically change current patterns and shape new global economic situations. First, Europe and the United States are quickly changing from stability to instability, having started with financial uncertainty, now moving to economic problems, and later even to political insecurity and social unrest if not contained. Africa, on the other hand, will become more stable and will be considered less risky in the future. The view of Africa compared to the rest of the world will balance out.

Second, while media still lags behind in sharing positive headlines about Africa, there is a shift to more holistic reporting. The more success stories that are told about Africa, the more potential investors will pay attention to Africa as an investment destination that is worth considering.

Third, more African political and economic leaders are promoting foreign direct investments instead of development aid. They want to attract serious businesses and sincere investors to their countries. Companies and entrepreneurs are offered many investment incentives.

The classic concept of helping poor African nations by granting credit and donating goods and money is not the Africa of today. For example, Nigerian President Goodluck Jonathan stated, at the G8 African Leaders Outreach at the G8/G20 Toronto Summit in June 2010, that his country would prefer removal of trade barriers over aid.

Therefore, development aid will successively be replaced by investments. In fact, the process is well underway. Foreign direct investment (FDI) to the continent reached $88 billion in 2008, according to the annual *African Economic Outlook.*[6] This was double the figure, provided by the Organization for Economic Co-operation and Development (OECD)[7], of $44 billion for net official development assistance (ODA) in 2008.

Fourth, today's Africa speaks for itself as a compelling investment case in six areas – macroeconomic stability and economic reform; low inclusion in world financial systems; fewer conflicts; abundant

---

[6] http://www.africaneconomicoutlook.org
[7] http://www.oecd.org

resources; a large, growing, under tapped consumer market; and a growing number of emerging versus developing economies.

Macroeconomic Stability and Economic Reform

This is the Central Bank of West African States in Bamako, Mali. (Photo by: Hartmut Sieper)

The macroeconomic situation is favorable. Short-, medium-, and long-term growth can be expected for most countries. Growth in Sub-Saharan Africa in 2010 is estimated at 5%, according to the International Monetary Fund (IMF).[8] In 2011, growth is forecast to reach 5.5%. Compare this to a growth forecast under 3% in Western

---

[8] http://www.imf.org

economies, according to the *Global Economic Prospects 2011*[9] by the World Bank. In fact, expectations for Sub-Saharan Africa's growth exceed those for global growth (3.3%) overall.

Also, governments have demonstrated strong commitment to economic reforms, which has resulted in improved legal frameworks for investors and companies. A good example is the introduction of one-stop shops that allow foreign investors to found companies in a few days, compared with the norm of several weeks or even months. In Rwanda, you only need three days to launch a company. To found a company in Botswana from Europe, one can do all the paperwork at the London office of the Botswana Export Development and Investment Agency (BEDIA).

Low Inclusion in the World's Financial Systems

Africa's low inclusion into the world's financial systems, which was considered negative in the past, is now revealed to be a blessing. Toxic assets have not found their way into balance sheets of most African banks. Asset price bubbles, fired by credit inflation, could not develop because of limited availability of loans and high interest rates. There is no excess liquidity in Africa that could have led to artificially high prices. Where asset prices are high, the main reason is a combination of elevated demand and lack of supply. Africa has shown an impressive robustness against the world financial and economic crisis.

---

[9] World Bank. (January 2011). Global Economic Prospects 2011. Accessed online at http://web.worldbank.org/WBSITE/EXTERNAL/EXTDEC/EXTDECPROSPECTS/GEPEXT/0,,contentMDK:22804791~pagePK:51087946~piPK:51087916~theSitePK:538110,00.html (January 20, 2011).

Note: Africa did experience varying levels of disruption in trade and investment due to the global economic crisis. However, these areas are on the rebound. As mentioned before, Sub-Saharan Africa is expected to experience broad-based growth in 2011 at about 5.5%.

Fewer Conflicts

The decline in political conflicts and wars makes Africa less risky. While the news still often reports of the eastern DRC, Somalia, and Sudan, as well as recent upheavals in Cote d'Ivoire, Tunisia, Egypt, Algeria, and Libya, investors should remember that these are a few out of 53 countries.

There is a strong trend towards democratic or open forms of government. Also, stronger institutions are on the rise.

Natural Resources

This is a copper facility in Zambia. (Photo by: Hartmut Sieper)

Africa's natural resources are not only abundant but diverse. A number of countries have many natural resources. For example, the DRC has abundant water, arable land, and dozens of different mineral resources, including gold, copper, uranium, diamonds, and coltan.

Many regions are severely under explored. Increased exploration activities may lead to positive surprises and unexpected results like the offshore oil fields in Ghana, as well as newly discovered coal deposits in Mozambique and diamond fields in Zimbabwe.

Large Consumer Markets

The African population grew to 1 billion in 2010 and will reach over 2 billion in 2050 while Western populations will shrink. The five largest countries in 2010 by population are Nigeria (152 million), Ethiopia (88 million), Egypt (80 million), DRC (71 million), and South Africa (49 million), according to *The World Factbook*.

Vijay Mahajan, author of *Africa Rising: How 900 Million African Consumers Offer More Than You Think*[10], says there is a large middle class with unmet needs in Africa. This middle class needs basic services like housing, energy, education, health, food, and transport. They have money to pay for it. They are unlike their Western counterparts who carry too much debt.

However, the African middle class, like other middle classes in developing countries, does not have average annual incomes upward of $30,000 like the Western middle class. On the other hand, the large, potential market can offset this for businesses and investors.

These consumer markets are also fragmented. Many countries have fewer than 5 million people. This is one reason why African countries are driving regional integration to enlarge the consumer

---

[10] Mahajan, V. (2008). *Africa Rising: How 900 Million African Consumers Offer More than You Think*. New Jersey: Pearson Prentice Hall.

markets. In fact, the East Africa Community (EAC) formed a common market in 2010 with a population of over 130 million. This makes it and its member countries – Rwanda, Burundi, Kenya, Uganda, and Tanzania - a market size on par with Nigeria.

Many Emerging Economies

The 70s, 80s, and early 90s signaled a decline in African economies with many becoming virtually bankrupt and indebted to foreign countries and international organizations like the IMF. Now, most of these countries have low debt and are growing well.

For about 15 years (prior to the economic crisis), 17 of the 53 African economies have maintained economic growth at more than 5% per year on average, according to Steve Radelet, author of *Emerging Africa: How 17 African Countries are Leading the Way.*[11] They have also added 3.2% GDP per capita per year. Some of these countries are Kenya, Mozambique, Tanzania, Uganda, and Ghana.

Ghana is an excellent example of the progress. It became a middle-income country in 2010. Also, it is on target to halve its poverty level by the end of 2015 in line with its Millennium Development Goals (MDGs).

Radelet notes that another six economies, such as Liberia and Sierra Leone, are headed to emerging economy status.

---

[11] Radelet, S. (2010). *Emerging Africa: How 17 African Countries are Leading the Way.* Washington, DC: Center for Global Development. (You can also listen to an interview conducted by Lauri Elliott with Steve Radelet at http://www.blogtalkradio.com/afribiz/2010/10/07/emerging-economies-in-africa-on-the-rise.)

Africa as an Epicenter of Global Trade

After the G20 meetings in Toronto in June 2010, it was very clear nations see a new era of a multi-polar world. Fareed Zakaria, host of CNN's GPS and author of *The Post-American World*[12], applied the concept of a multi-polar world to politics, or nation states. In essence, the world agenda will no longer be dominated by one or a few nations. Political power will be dispersed more broadly.

In a report by Accenture called *The Rise of the Multi-Polar World*[13], it says that global economic power will no longer reside with the United States, Europe, and Japan. It will disperse as "developing economies contribute an ever-increasing share of the world's output, trade and investment." In fact, developing countries are expected to account for 2/3 of global trade in 2050, according to *The World Order in 2050*[14] policy outlook by Uri Dadush and Bennett Stancil.

In the backdrop of these dynamics, seemingly, is Africa. With little representation in the G20, reduced votes in the International Monetary Fund, and perhaps not enough impact in other international organizations like the United Nations and World Health Organization, it would seem Africa is a loser in this new era.

But political and economic dynamics are not the only things changing. Forms of influence and power are also changing. Power is also dispersing among spheres of society, who are interconnected. The most common spheres are business, social, and government. However, today these spheres are overlaid with transnational networks, global policy networks, advocacy networks, value networks, social networks gone viral, etc. This will result in influence

---

[12] Zakaria, F. (2009). *The Post-American World*. New York, NY: W.W. Norton & Company.
[13] Accenture. (2007). The Rise of the Multi-Polar World.
[14] Dadush, U., & Stancil, B. (2010). The World Order in 2050. *Policy Outlook*. Carnegie Endowment for International Peace.

and power emerging in new and different forms, allowing more diverse and unique ways of articulating and acting upon influence and power.

While Africa may seem to be losing ground in some formal arenas, it may have gained ground where it matters – economics. And because new and different forms of influence and power are emerging, Africa will be able to find ways to leverage its growing economic influence.

The shape of Africa's growing economic influence is centered on two areas – being a pole of growth and an epicenter of trade. With solid economic performance, abundant natural resources, and a large consumer market, Africa is on a path to be one of the poles, or regions, of growth in spite of Sub-Saharan Africa having the predominate number of Least Development Countries (LDCs).

The other area in Africa's growing economic influence has not been clearly articulated or stressed. Africa is positioned as an epicenter and gateway for global business and trade. This has quietly snuck up on the world while the world was focused on the economic crisis.

If you look at the number of trade agreements being introduced between Africa and the rest of the world at this time (e.g., between the United States and Angola, between China and many African states, between India, Brazil, and South Africa), you will see that they are increasing and expanding. In the last few years, heads of states from around the world, e.g., Iran, Russia, Brazil, United States, France, have visited Africa to improve diplomatic and economic ties.

These activities do not occur unless there are significant benefits sought by these nations. It's obvious that Africa has something the world wants. During the Cold War era, Africa served as a geopolitical map of opposing political ideologies between the U.S. and Soviet Union. But now, the primary focus is economic, because strong economies bolster governments, those in office, communities, and citizens. This is not to ignore other benefits that countries might seek, like cultural exchange, from ties with African nations.

Also, there is increased south south and developing country cooperation, which means trade and business flows are moving in new directions. The developing economies that will lead global trade in 2050 are increasingly trading among themselves, but not to the exclusion of developed countries. In this, Africa is increasingly part of the engagement. Look at the India, Brazil, South Africa (IBSA) Forum activities, the China-Africa Forum activities, and the Southern African Customs Union's (SACU) preferential trade agreement with the Southern Common Market (MERCOSUR) as examples.

In this context, Africa's rising economic influence will translate to more political influence, which may be "soft" more than formal in the short to medium term. For example, Nicolas Sarkozy, President of France, held the 25th annual Africa-France Summit in 2010, which focused not on politics but on business. At the summit, Sarkozy said he would call for an expanded role of African nations in the United Nations when he heads the G20 this year. And also, Canadian Prime Minister Stephen Harper personally invited additional African leaders like President Goodluck Jonathan of Nigeria and African Union Chairperson Bingu wa Mutharika to attend the G20 Toronto Summit in 2010 in recognition of the need to include the region.

But another primary benefit of these political and economic processes is that Africa will serve as a global trade epicenter and gateway into other emerging markets, and even into developed nations. Africa has the ability to be a bridge to enter into other markets, as well as a key location for global value chains.

U.S. Honeywell has taken its Chinese connections to enter the Sub-Saharan African market, so why couldn't firms use Africa to enter other regions because of Africa's increasingly favorable ties? In another instance, Chinese firms are partnering with African governments to establish economic zones and manufacturing capacity in Africa based on the experience of economic zones in China. This will create capacity for these firms to serve China's domestic market and the African consumer markets in the future.

And finally, the question of "How well is Africa positioned to be an epicenter and gateway of global trade?" comes to mind. Africa still faces many hard realities like poverty, lack of infrastructure, unemployment, and instability in some countries, but other developing nations also face the same or similar issues. And, for the most part, African countries have proven to be economically and politically resistant to instability in the last decade. Governance and the business climate have also improved while conflicts have reduced dramatically.

But in truth, Africa does not need everything in place, but it does need enough significant leverage points to take advantage of this position and use them to create a tipping point to solidly establish and maintain this position. As indicated before, the increasing diplomatic and economic ties between Africa and the rest of the world, its natural resources, and large, growing consumer markets are key leverage points.

Another leverage point is the image of Africa, which is changing. The successful conclusion of the FIFA World Cup in South Africa perhaps helped to produce a tipping point.

And one leverage point not used enough is that there are pockets in Africa, South Africa and Mauritius for example, where business is run on par, in many facets, with the world. In fact, there are many more places where this is the case because of economic zones. An economic zone, such as a free trade zone or export–processing zone, generally has a good climate, procedures, infrastructure, business support, laws, and incentives conducive for business, even when the country in which it is located does not. And if you dig a little deeper, you will find more significant leverage points.

A Look at South Africa's Recent Strategic Moves

2010 was a major year for South Africa with the successful FIFA World Cup. However significant the event, it pales to the global political positioning South Africa has worked for itself in the past year. It is obvious the government continues to learn more about how to use the country's strategic, not just natural, assets to secure its position globally. Hopefully, this will help South Africa economically in the future.

In 2010, President Zuma visited each of the BRIC (Brazil, Russia, India, and China) countries to cement and increase both political and economic ties. The recent result is South Africa being approved as a member by BRIC member nations, so effectively BRIC becomes BRICS.

It's also important to remember what BRIC actually represents. In *The World Needs Better Economic BRICs*[15], Jim O'Neill of Goldman Sachs coined the phrase, BRIC, referring to the countries in terms of their advancing stage of economic development as emerging economies. Goldman Sachs projects they may economically overtake the richest nations by 2050. China has already headed down this path by overtaking Japan and Germany in the last year to rank as the world's 2nd largest economy.

---

[15] O'Neill, J. (2001). The World Needs Better Economic BRICS. *Global Economics: Paper No. 66.* Goldman Sachs. Available online at http://www2.goldmansachs.com/ideas/brics/building-better-doc.pdf.

Goldman Sachs has more recently presented a second series of nations it believes will arise called N11, including Egypt, Nigeria, and Vietnam. South Africa does not appear on either of Goldman Sachs' lists.

South Africa does appear on two other emerging economies lists – CIVETS (Colombia, Indonesia, Vietnam, Egypt, Turkey, and South Africa) and MAVINS (Mexico, Australia, Vietnam, Indonesia, Nigeria, and South Africa). So, there is recognition of potential but what remains at issue is how will South Africa continue to progress for the long term when its medium-term economic prospects are sluggish?

Even though O'Neill says that South Africa is not the best choice for the next BRIC because of the size of its consumer market and struggling economy, it was chosen anyway by the current BRIC. How is that? South Africa has become better at leveraging its assets strategically and being a BRIC is no longer just about economics but also geopolitics.

While these designations - BRIC, N11, CIVETS, and MAVIN - are only descriptors and do not represent any formal economic bloc, the BRIC nations have formed an alliance to increase their geopolitical influence seeing as they already represent more than half the world's global growth. Accepting South Africa as a BRIC, demonstrates the importance the BRICs place on Africa going into the future and possibly South Africa's ability to help further ties with the rest of the continent. So, South Africa has been accepted geopolitically, but not necessarily economically, as a BRIC.

This occurrence aligns with the insights I (Lauri) shared previously in the article, *Africa Positioned as an Epicenter of Global Trade.*[16] I wrote about Africa's new position as a global business, trade, and investment hub. While at work for some time, the global recession made the transformation more apparent although we hear more about Africa's problems than its economic accomplishments, which include having low levels of government debt that should make the U.S. and many European countries drool.

Speaking of South Africa specifically, it is a member of the G20 nations, which are supposed to work together to coordinate policies that impact global economics. In 2011, South Africa will take a two-year, non-permanent member rotation on the UN Security Council, effectively replacing Uganda which has held a position for the last two years. And it is likely that South Africa will gain more votes in the International Monetary Fund within the next two years as the IMF shifts 6% more voting power to emerging markets.

Along with still being the largest economy in Africa, these dynamics will no doubt give South Africa the ability to yield more of what U.S. Secretary of State Clinton calls "smart power." But what South Africa needs out of this more than anything else is the economic benefit.

South Africa's trade with the United States and European Union combined still exceeds over 30%, although China as a country is now the largest trade partner with South Africa. Economic recovery in the U.S. and Europe is expected to slow in 2011, and South Africa's economic recovery is expected to slow as well. In essence, South Africa does not expect to experience broad-based growth, which the IMF projects for Sub-Saharan Africa in 2011.

---

[16] Elliott, L. (July 15, 2010). Africa Positioned as an Epicenter of Global Trade. *Afribiz.net.* Located online at http://www.afribiz.net/content/africa-positioned-as-an-epicenter-of-global-trade.

While there are many reasons South Africa would seek strong ties with the existing BRICs, the fact that at least India and China are expected to have strong growth rates over the next few years presents an opportunity for stimulating South Africa's economy through trade with the existing BRICs. In the long run, the BRIC consumer markets present increased opportunities just on sheer size. South Africa has the smallest consumer market of the soon-to-be BRICS alliance with approximately 50 million people. This compares to approximately 139 million people in Russia, 200 million people in Brazil, 1.1 billion people in India, and 1.3 billion in China.[17]

Even with economic struggles, South Africa is still an emerging economy and the BRICS designation will help the country continue to transform its brand image positively. South Africa will also find preferential trade status within BRICS, which was already well underway and opens more doors for South African businesses and investors.

And finally, South Africa represents the strongest formal flows of information, resources, investment, trade, and business on the continent. If you operate or have strong partnerships in South Africa, it opens doors to south south trade flows not just north south trade flows. And it's the south south and African regional trade flows that will become increasingly important over the next few decades.

Note: *Africa is not the only emerging region which the Lord will bless with wealth. God is looking out for Asia, including India, China, Vietnam, as well as Latin America. What makes Africa unique is that it is by far the underdog, which will surprise many in the coming years.*

---

[17] Central Intelligence Agency. (2010). *The World Factbook.* Accessed online at https://www.cia.gov/library/publications/the-world-factbook/index.html (December 2010).

Africa's reach will be likened to Cyrus of Persia's quick sweep (Isaiah 41:1-5) to take over the empire and spread it beyond its original boundaries. And because the Church is one of the key networks on the continent, we will be at the center of it. It won't be empire as history describes, but an empire of influence.

Transforming Our Minds about Doing Business in Africa

Perception has emerged as a powerful influence in today's economic world. Economic activities are highly influenced by perceived risk in a geographic area. It is widely acknowledged that Africa suffers a negative perception of itself and from the view point of foreign investors. Many people have been typically sold a picture of a totally non-functional Africa. Africa is known for wildlife, poverty and disease, and for being a major aid recipient.

Amidst its complexities, Africa offers valid opportunity for investments, vibrant communities, citizens eager for change, a growing market, fast changing laws, a transforming society, etc. It is the next frontier for growth and development. This includes business.

Business is highly influenced by perception also, and hence it is fundamental that the perception towards Africa is addressed as a first step towards doing business on the continent. There are certain long standing paradigms that have dogged the continent. Provided below is a new frame for new mindsets.

New Mindset: Help the Poor by Helping the Rich

The current paradigm says that all Africans are poor and desperately need help. Mahajan, author of *Africa Rising*, provides estimates that say there are about 450 million people living below the poverty level. However, Africa has about a billion people. This means there's another 450 to 500 million who can afford goods and services.

Additional estimates shared by Mahajan place the African middle class at about 150 million people, who are able to purchase goods at par with the rest of the world. This is equivalent to India's middle class. Focus needs to be placed on growing the wealthier 450 million as a strategy towards lifting the poorer 450 million out of poverty.

This new shift will create a virtuous cycle, i.e., invest in businesses that provide goods and services for the wealthier 450 million, thus creating jobs for the lower 450 million. These 450 million people will eventually move up the economic scale, demanding and able to afford more goods and services.

This model is similar to what has happened in China over the past twenty to thirty years, creating the world's biggest economic upliftment. This moved hundreds of millions of people from poverty.

New Mindset: Reduce Poverty through Small Business

The current paradigm says that creating enterprise is not as important as aid. Fortunately, we are on the nexus of this paradigm shift.

African poverty can be greatly reduced through micro, small, and medium enterprises (SMMEs). These are the engines of economic growth for countries globally. Small businesses create more jobs than any other entity. Because of the African communal lifestyle, every single job created through small businesses affects at least four lives. In some African contexts, the ratio is greater.

New Mindset: A Transformed Purpose for Aid

Aid on its own cannot eradicate poverty. Aid should be an emergency measure targeted especially at severe, distressed sectors. It should also focus on sectors which do not easily and immediately attract investors. However, it should not become a permanent feature.

Also, donor agencies, aid agencies, and mission organizations need to actively re-tool their model towards Africa. They should channel at least 25% of their funding into sustainable business investments. They can still be focused on the communities in which they traditionally serve.

New Mindset: Transfer Responsibility

The current paradigm is that Africa cannot solve its problems, and is perpetually dependent on foreign solutions. In actuality, Africa can solve most of its problems internally. Where foreign aid organizations bring help, it should be complementary.

Such bodies and agencies should target turning their current recipients into donors within a ten-year period. Repeating this process will subsequently reduce poverty and transfer the responsibility of wealth creation squarely into the hands of the Africans themselves.

New Mindset: Africans Themselves Want Change

The current paradigm is that Africans are passive and beggarly. However, there is an increasing demand by Africans for trade rather than aid.

This desire is reflected both in the government and private sector. Presidents like Yoweri Museveni of Uganda are quoted as requesting more trade, not aid. Paul Kagame, President of Rwanda, has launched a national program to shift the mindset of his nation away from aid. This mindset is increasingly spreading across the continent.

New Mindset: Increased Investment in the Private Sector Improves Governance

The current paradigm is Africa is all about bad governance, and that only a change in governance can change things. This means the focus is on politics and governance.

There is a saying that he who pays the piper dictates the tune. When businesses are empowered, they are able to affect governance in the long run. They become stronger, growing into tax payers and hence influencers. They have a voice and sooner or later government listens to them. For example, the Nigerian government some time ago set up a committee of over 300 of its leading business people to craft business laws aimed at propelling its economy in the next ten years.

On the other hand, when a government's chief source of income is foreign aid, it dances to the tune of foreign donors, which at times is at the expense of its local private sector. It is not motivated to listen to its people.

New Mindset: Business is Already Doing a Lot

The current paradigm is businesses in Africa are only greedy and exploitative. In truth, many successful African businesses have already taken up significant levels of social responsibility, including projects like fighting disease, sponsoring education, and developing community projects.

Through these companies, many have received aid from local sources. In a Lesotho clothing factory, staff has its maternity and other hospital needs covered by clinics sponsored by the company. In South Africa, staff is allowed to recommend social projects into which businesses invest. In some parts of the continent, companies send out staff to help in community projects like building houses. These help prove that business will play a huge role in solving the problems and is already doing so.

New Mindset: Africa Offers Unlimited Business Opportunities

The current paradigm is there are few profitable opportunities in Africa. Actually, almost every type of business operating in Africa shows profitability. Because most African countries have low development thresholds, there is huge demand in almost every sector. This is unlike many Western markets, which have become saturated.

New Mindset: There is Money to be Made

The current paradigm is there is no money to be made. People are poor and cannot afford goods and services. Many African countries benefited from the resource boom of the last few years, before the collapse of 2008. Many of these are awash with cash.

For example, Nigeria drove its foreign reserves from $7 billion in 2001 to about $63 billion in 2008. Today, those reserves are at about $33 billion. The country is planning to set up a sovereign wealth fund with a view to finding lucrative opportunities to invest its wealth.

African countries need help to avoid capital flight by helping communities produce most of their consumer needs, such as food, clothing, and housing. These are only more opportunities for entrepreneurs.

New Mindset: There is Risk Involved, but a Commensurate High Rate of Return

The current paradigm is that Africa is simply too risky. Its political tensions at times, weak judicial systems, and certain unstable societies seem not to offer any attraction to some investors. However, the truth is that the return on investment in Africa far outstrips what is possible from most other regions. Many people refer to these returns as a "well-hidden secret" that has been beneficial to a few business people.

Africa has its risks, and they abound. Businesses open up and shut down for one reason or the other. This is not exclusive to Africa. The global business failure rate is not far different from what it is in Africa.

Conclusion

Africa has been shrouded in darkness for many centuries. In fact, maps charting the amount of light generated around the world have shown Africa to be much darker than most of the world.

But this is no longer the case, because Africa's time to arise and shine has come (Isaiah 60). Africa has been positioned now to reap the harvest of its assets. This chapter focused on illustrating how Africa is making great strides economically while increasing influence geopolitically, which reveals the unveiling of the "Africa Rising" prophetic mantle over the continent.

Many will be joyous that the burden of Africa and its people is finally lifting. But on the other hand, some Christians, particularly in the United States and the West, find it alarming that political and economic influence is shifting elsewhere. In fact, many respond with fear, control, and manipulation to keep things as they are.

Shifting political and economic power doesn't mean others will dominate, but it does mean there will be a re-balancing globally. And remember, it is the Lord's Kingdom that is to reign supremely over creation not man-made institutions or governments.

We can be encouraged by the Word, which says, "Of the increase of His government and of peace there shall be no end..." (Amplified Bible, Isaiah 9:7). In Revelation 11:15, it speaks of the kingdoms of the world becoming the kingdoms of Christ. And in Daniel 7:18, it says that the saints will receive and possess the Kingdom forever.

So, if God has richly blessed Africa and positioned it to exert more influence globally, as well as placed the Church as a significant stakeholder on the continent, we as the body of Christ are also well positioned globally and will reap the blessings and benefits of our partnerships in Africa. And our web of influence can only increase with our bond with Africa.

We need to be ready to act on the opportunities God has given each one of us when the time comes. Take what we have shared to the Lord in prayer and let Him both illuminate and transform your mind, as well as reveal strategies and practices for your own use and to His glory.

3

Glaring Opportunities:
Urbanization, Agriculture, and ICT

Hartmut Sieper

Nissi Ekpott

Lauri Elliott

Africa is a vast continent with vast and different opportunities. There are well developed sectors in Africa like oil in Nigeria, mining in South Africa, and mobile communication in several different parts of the continent. However, most of its countries are low-income countries, which rely on primary sectors like mining and agriculture. This means there are astounding opportunities as the countries continue to develop in secondary (e.g., manufacturing), tertiary (e.g., services), and quaternary (e.g., intellectual) sectors. Even key primary sectors are underdeveloped in many countries, providing enormous opportunities.

Africa's natural assets are its natural resources and people. On these assets, the foundation for economic development and business opportunities exist. For example, in the next decade there will be a push for commodities – minerals, oil, and agricultural products – which Africa has in abundance. If these sectors drive broad-based growth, including jobs for people, consumers will continue to move up the socioeconomic scale and diversify their consumption patterns.

There are five opportunities we decided to share with you out of the enumerable opportunities on the continent – urbanization, agriculture, ICT, gold, and consumers. The first three are covered in this chapter while gold and consumers each have their own chapter.

Urbanization

Urbanization is one of the big megatrends in the world of today and tomorrow. Millions of people are migrating from rural to urban areas for many reasons. While the percentage of people living in urban areas has already reached very high levels in the Western world and Latin America, some parts of Asia and most parts of Africa are lagging behind.

The urban population in Africa accounts for about 40% of the continent's total population. In Latin America, a similar proportion between urban and rural population was observed in 1950. Within the next decade, more than 80% of all Latin Americans will live in cities.[18] So, Africa lies 60 years behind Latin America if it follows the same trajectory.

The urban population growth in Africa is mainly determined by two major factors: the migration of mostly young people from rural to urban areas, and high general population growth because of high fertility rates and low median ages. And because Africa's youth bulge is now reaching adulthood and will move to cities for better opportunities, Africa will quickly catch up with Latin America.

---

[18] UN-HABITAT. (2010). The State of African Cities 2010: Governance, Inequalities and Urban Land Markets. Accessed online at http://www.unhabitat.org/documents/SACR-ALL-10-FINAL.pdf (January 8, 2011).

According to UN-HABITAT, Africa will experience the strongest urban population growth among all regions of the world until 2050. From 2000 to 2030, Africa's urban population will grow from 294 million to 742 million people, an increase of 152%. In comparison, the urban population in Asia will grow by 94%, while Latin America will add another 55%.

The three largest cities in Africa are Cairo (Egypt), Lagos (Nigeria), and Kinshasa (DRC).[19] Cairo and Lagos populations exceed 10 million making them megacities.

In about 10 years, Cairo will be overtaken by Lagos and Kinshasa. Many African cities will have grown more than 50% between 2006 and 2020. The image on the following page shows the largest and fastest growing cities in Africa.

---

[19] In other sources, Johannesburg, South Africa is in the top three largest cities in Africa because the East Rand is incorporated into the figures. The UN-HABITAT figures here separate the two.

Rabat
Casablanca
Algier
Tripoli

Dakar

Khartoum

Bamako
Kaduna   Kano
Conakry
Ibadan
Addis Ababa
Douala
Abidjan   Accra **Lagos**
Yaounde   Kampala   Nairobi
Mogadishu

Size (2020e):

○   1 – 3 mn

○   3 – 5 mn

○   5 – 10 mn

○   > 10 mn

Brazzaville   Kinshasa
Luanda   Lubumbashi
Dar es-Salaam

Growth 2006- 2020:

▨   70 – 85 %

▨   50 – 69 %

▢   30 – 49 %

▢   < 30 %

Lusaka

Pretoria   Antananarivo
Johannesburg   Maputo
East Rand

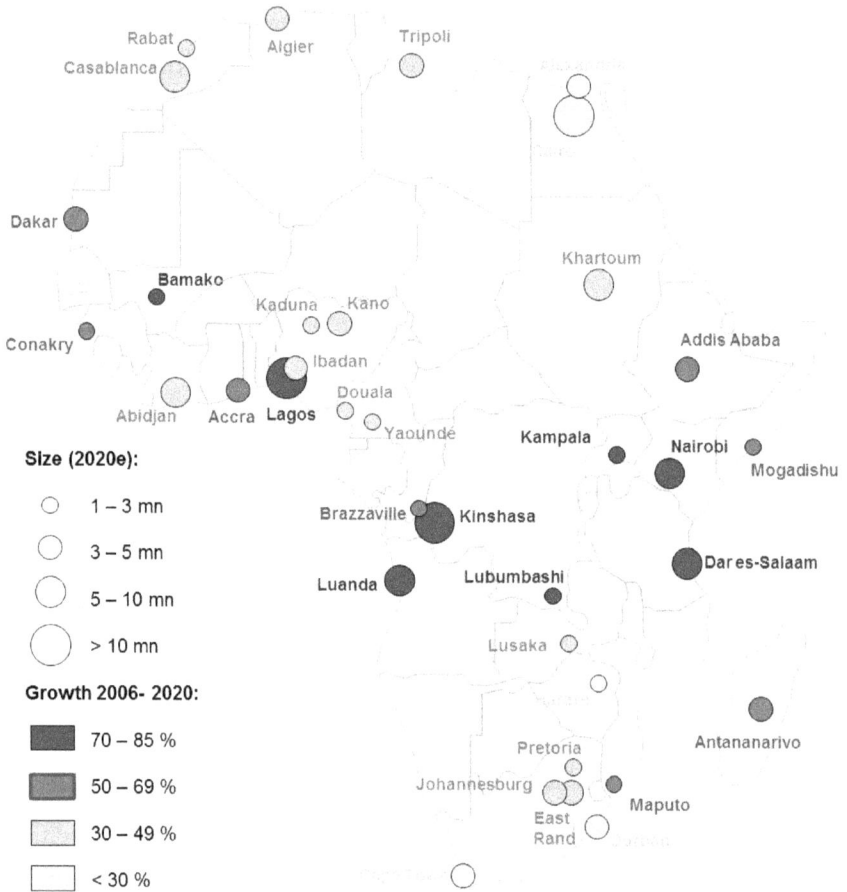

Source: Trans Africa Invest, based on data of CityMayors

Another factor influencing urbanization is how densely populated a country is. The small countries of Rwanda and Burundi have already passed levels of sustainability regarding the ability to feed their own people with agricultural goods from local sources. Too many people are living too close to each other, allowing only very small parcels of agricultural land per family. Fertile grounds in this country are almost utilized by 100%, so that there is no further expansion possible.

As a result of this unpleasant situation, many young people are forced to leave their parents' farms and will move into the cities looking for a job, or any informal business activity, that will allow them to earn a living.

Urbanization will definitely accelerate in those countries. Right now, more than 80% of the overall population of the East African countries of Rwanda, Burundi, Uganda, and Ethiopia is still living in rural areas. Consequently, rapid growth of the primary cities of those countries can be anticipated with very high probability.

Uganda is an excellent example for the extreme dynamics of future urban growth. The country has one of the youngest populations worldwide. Regarding fertility (6.73 children born per woman) and birthrate (47.55 births /1,000 population), Uganda is ranked second, according to the World Factbook. The population growth rate is approximately 3.6% per year, according to 2010 estimates. The median age is 15, which means that half the population is younger than 15 years. One can anticipate the transformation of this high youth population - from too young to being productive citizens; from a burden to a benefit when the majority of youth reach adulthood. What is called the "demographic dividend" will begin to pay off.

One can easily imagine the future exponential growth of urban areas. In 2008, only 13% of Ugandans were living in cities. Over the next 20 years, the urban population will well exceed the 20% level, leading to rapid growth of the capital city of Kampala, which is also the economic and financial center of the country.

The rapid growth of African cities will both imply major problems and create outstanding opportunities. The challenges are obvious. They range from infrastructure gaps and missing capacities for power, water, and food supply to loss of agricultural land and chaotic traffic situations, not to mention the huge health problems originating from air pollution, lack of sanitation, and huge piles of garbage.

Harare, Zimbabwe: Offers good value for investors because of depressed asset prices as a result of the 2009 currency reform and political uncertainties. (Photo by: Hartmut Sieper)

Clever entrepreneurs, who understand problems are also opportunities, will find a large variety of promising business concepts by proactively dealing with the aforementioned challenges in city development in Africa. Sophisticated city planning methods, innovative waste management procedures, cost efficient water treatment technologies, and independent power plants belong to this category of opportunities.

Studying past history reveals another set of opportunities. When we look back to urban expansion in Western countries, we find some business cases that should work in Africa as well. Land prices will increase when the plots move closer to the city. Many farmers in Europe became millionaires just because their farmland was converted into building land.

From an investor's point of view, we will take a look at some glaring opportunities that are connected with the megatrend of urbanization in Africa. There is a significant unsatisfied need in residential housing in all major African cities. The gap between demand and supply is still increasing, offering numerous opportunities for real estate developers, prefab house suppliers, and construction companies.

The market environment is completely different from the situation that we are familiar with in the Western economies. An example is if you want to rent a flat in some cities like Lagos, Douala, or Luanda, you have to pay the rent for up to 24 months in advance. For real estate developers, such down payments from future renters will provide a solid base for financing ventures.

However, it is not so easy to tap into this kind of business opportunity. In practical terms, it can be very difficult, costly, and time-consuming to get the necessary licenses for starting operations. Corruption is known to exist. Securing and maintaining ownership rights might also be difficult, depending on the rule of law, the availability and reliability of title deeds, and the handling process in general.

The more well developed real estate markets are found in North Africa, including Egypt and Morocco, Cape Verde, and South Africa to name a few. Because they are more developed, rates of return may not be as high though. There are online resources to help decipher the investment and business climate related to land across countries.[20]

In some countries, where there is no private ownership of urban land possible, lease holds can be obtained for a period of 25, 49, or even 99 years. In many countries, leasing is the only possibility of getting agricultural land. However, lease rates can be very inexpensive and be negotiated for a long period. This might be very attractive for long-term investors.

Lagos, Nigeria: There is a never-ending construction boom. (Photo by: Hartmut Sieper)

Investors that want to find out which cities would offer the best development perspective and the biggest potential for future price increases would have to look for a number of parameters. The most important factor is location. This is true for selecting the right

---

[20] For example, visit the International Finance Corporation's websites – http://www.investingacrossborders.org and http://www.doingbusiness.org.

strategic location, i.e., in which city the property should be bought, as well as choosing the right quarter within the city. If you intend to buy property outside the big cities in order to benefit from lower prices, there should be a positive outlook for future development.

Selecting locations along important national, or transnational, development corridors is a good idea. Examples of these corridors are:

- Johannesburg/Pretoria – Nelspruit – Maputo
- Johannesburg – Durban
- Johannesburg – Gaborone – Francistown – Bulawayo – Gweru – Kadoma – Harare
- Harare – Mutare – Beira
- Harare – Lusaka – Ndola – Lubumbashi
- Lagos – Porto Novo – Lome – Accra – Takoradi – Abidjan
- Luanda – Kinshasa/Brazzaville – Libreville – Douala
- Douala – Yaounde – Bangui – Ndjamena
- Mombasa – Nairobi – Kampala
- Kampala – Entebbe

Along these major transnational road connections, many business opportunities will emerge. Truckers want to eat and to sleep. Commuters will visit shopping centers. Minibuses will stop at many places along the road. Those highly frequented places are good locations to sell goods and services. The overland roads carry further business opportunities like public transportation, logistics services, international border controls, and road construction and maintenance.

Rapidly growing cities will accommodate an increasing number of inhabitants, workers, and consumers. If everything goes right, prices should increase and all stakeholders would be able to prosper.

However, African reality might be different. As long as economic growth is outpaced by demographic growth, income per capita will decrease, which will lead to more poverty. Reaching the millennium goal of poverty alleviation is only possible when economic growth is superior. This is the major reason why high economic growth over a long period of time is an essential prerequisite for sustainable development in Africa. Good governance, business friendly reforms, a reliable financial and fiscal environment, and political stability are needed to initiate, support, and sustain this process. And as indicated in Chapter 2 - *The New Africa*, Africa has demonstrated good progress in these areas for the last 15 years or so as a whole.

Air Traffic Patterns and Cities

An interesting question is, which large cities will benefit most from globalization and intraregional trade? We can use air traffic patterns and growth to draw some insights. In Sub-Saharan Africa, the major international airport in Johannesburg, O.R. Tambo, is by far the most frequented one, followed by those in Nairobi and Addis Ababa. In the long term, the importance of Johannesburg should decrease because other destinations like Luanda, Lusaka, and Harare will increase in importance, thus allowing passengers from Europe to get to Angola, Zambia, and Zimbabwe directly instead of transferring at Johannesburg.

On the other hand, the future of Addis Ababa should be bright. The capital city of Ethiopia, the third most populous African country, is ideally located as a strategic gateway from Asia to Africa. Recognizing this competitive advantage, Ethiopian Airlines has already opened new flight routes from Addis Ababa to China and India. It can be anticipated that Addis Ababa will grow significantly over the next decade, since this city is centrally located and by far the biggest and most important urbanized area in Ethiopia.

Urbanization Impact on Construction

As indicated before, the construction sector is a key business and investment opportunity. New city dwellers need appropriate housing facilities according to their financial power. Upper, middle, and lower class residential houses are in high demand in almost all African cities. In Angola alone, one million houses are needed - this for a country with a total population of only 13 million people.

The Angolan government is actively pursuing a gigantic house building program and is looking for construction companies and experienced real estate developers that can handle complex operations and deliver several thousand units at the same time. Lack of financing is the biggest problem in this sphere of business, along with high levels of corruption. However, there are ways to navigate these environments as well. For example, the U.S. has a bilateral agreement with Angola covering trade and investment, which offers certain levels of support and protection for U.S. companies.[21]

Of all the subsectors in residential housing, low-cost housing is the most challenging because of high-volume, low-margin operations, but the rewards can be very high. The environment of the construction business in Africa is very different from the situation in the U.S. and many European countries: there is no oversupply, no real estate price bubbles, and definitely not a decrease in demand. Instead, there is enough to do for thousands of companies over several decades. It's incredible, but it's true.

---

[21] For U.S. citizens, contact the U.S. Commercial Services and check out their market research reports at http://www.export.gov.

Agriculture

Agriculture in Africa offers many diverse opportunities. This is one area where Africa can have a competitive advantage over every other continent for some of the following basic reasons:

- Agriculture is ingrained in the culture; over 60% of Africans are already involved in farming, though largely subsistence.
- There is an abundance of arable land estimated at a potential of over 300 million hectares, according to the Food Agriculture Organization (FAO).
- The climate is largely favorable.
- There is access to water.
- Africa can meet diverse agricultural requirements.
- There is a market right in Africa - local consumption currently far outstrips production.
- There are relatively low labor costs.

Potential Arable Land and Market Size

Citing an FAO study, the UNEP/GRID Arendal website says that there is a potential of 300 million hectares of rain-fed, arable land above current availability.[22] This would be a potential increase anywhere from 150% to 750%. The greatest potential is in Southern Africa. (See graph on next page.)

---

[22] UNEP/GRID-Arendal. Current and Potential Arable Land Use in Africa. *UNEP/GRID-Arendal Maps and Graphics Library.* Accessed online at http://maps.grida.no/go/graphic/current_and_potential_arable_land_use_in_africa (January 11, 2011).

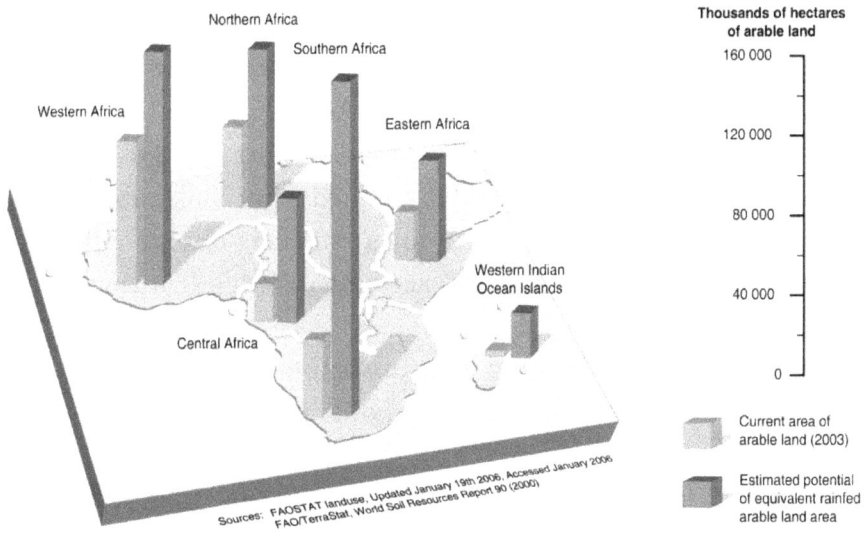

Source: Hugo Ahlenius, UNEP/GRID-Arendal

McKinsey estimates that Africa's agricultural sector currently generates crops valued at $280 billion each year.[23] It believes this could grow to $500 billion in 2020 and as much as $880 billion in 2030.

The vast market opportunities come first from meeting the needs of the large, local population. Many African nations are currently net importers of food, spending billions of dollars on food imports yearly. For instance, FAO reports that Nigeria imported $2.5-$2.7 billion in agricultural products between 2005 and 2007. Much of this food requirement can be produced locally.[24]

---

[23] McKinsey Global Institute. (2010). Lions on the Move: The Progress and Potential of African Economies. Accessed online at http://www.mckinsey.com/mgi/publications/progress_and_potential_of_african_ec onomies/pdfs/MGI_african_economies_full_report.pdf (January 11, 2011).

[24] Food and Agriculture Organization. (2009). *FAO Statistical Yearbook 2009.* Accessed online at http://www.fao.org/economic/ess/publications-studies/statistical-yearbook/fao-statistical-yearbook-2009/en (January 11, 2011).

Exports and Foreign Involvement in African Farmland

The FAO estimates that Africa's total agricultural exports reached a little over $25 billion in 2007.[25] According to the OECD Development Centre, "The agricultural export composition has experienced a major shift. It has diversified from bulk commodities to horticultural products and, to a smaller extent, processed products...."[26] However, Africa accounted for less than 3% of agricultural exports globally.

But think about it, this is a huge opportunity. Food consumption is expected to rise globally and Africa holds about 60% of the world's unused arable land.

In fact, the focus on African agriculture has accelerated tremendously in the past few years, following the trend where foreign governments, international agribusinesses, investment banks, hedge funds, commodity traders, sovereign wealth funds, as well as pension funds, foundations, and individuals are acquiring African land for the purpose of producing food for export.

This is probably by far the biggest single trend involving African agriculture in recent times. Rich nations currently hold millions of hectares of African farmland in a bid to tackle food shortages.

One example is Saudi Star in Ethiopia as reported in The Guardian.[27] Saudi Star has huge facilities, which pack 50 tons of food a day for export to markets in the Middle East. It currently employs over 1,000 women.

-----

[25] This figure does not include Djibouti, which did not appear in the FAO Statistical Yearbook 2009 data.

[26] Development Centre of the OECD. (2008). Business for Development 2008: Promoting Commercial Agriculture in Africa.

[27] Vidal, S. (March 7, 2010). How Food and Water are Driving a 21st-CenturyAfrican Land Grab. *The Guardian*. Accessed online at http://www.guardian.co.uk/environment/2010/mar/07/food-water-africa-land-grab. (February 10, 2011).

Though its benefits to Africans are still being debated in many quarters, the foreign interest is contributing to an increase in the value of agriculture on the continent. Analysts from Neuafrika.com believe that if this foreign supply is well balanced with local supply, it will add to creating an even larger potential market for agricultural products. Also, if properly handled, it will continue to bring in investment funds, technology, and create jobs. If poorly handled, it has the potential to become another form of colonization.

Land "Gold" Rush

Susan Payne, Chief Executive Officer of Emergent Asset Management, believes that farmland in Africa is giving a 25% return for investors while inviting billions of dollars in foreign investments.[28] It is also believed that these investments serve to uplift and provide jobs for locals.

Ethiopia is not the only African country involved in the land "rush." This land rush was triggered by the worldwide food shortages. The food shortages followed the sharp rise in the price of crude oil in 2008, increasing shortages of water, and new EU policies which stipulate that by the year 2015, 10% of all transport fuel must come from plant-based biofuels.

The first megadeal was announced in 2008 when the South Korean company, Daewoo Logistics, wanted to acquire 2.5 million hectares, equal to one half of the entire arable land of Madagascar. However, the deal was canceled by the new government of Madagascar after the coup of 2009. Some other foreign land deals include:

- Indian companies, backed by government loans, have bought or leased hundreds of thousands of hectares in Ethiopia,

---

[28] Ibid.

Kenya, Madagascar, Senegal, and Mozambique, where they are growing rice, sugar cane, maize, and lentils to feed their domestic market.

- In Sudan, South Korean companies recently bought 700,000 hectares in northern Sudan for wheat cultivation; the United Arab Emirates acquired 750,000 hectares; and Saudi Arabia has a 42,000-hectare deal in the Nile province.
- European biofuel companies have acquired or requested about 3.9 million hectares of land in Africa.
- Saudi Arabia earmarked $5 billion to provide loans at preferential rates to Saudi companies, which want to invest in countries with strong agricultural potential.

Note: *While it is not yet known if this rush will be beneficial or detrimental to Africa as a prophetic people, we have already seen in Isaiah 60 where the Lord promises to bring huge resources into Africa, creating new value out of what seemed rejected and valueless. I (Nissi) believe these land deals can completely transform Africa in an amazing way.*

Foreigners are not alone in taking advantage of Africa's agricultural potential. South African farmers secured 500,000 hectares of land in the Republic of Congo (Brazzaville) to farm for both export and local consumption. These farmers are following the global trend of securing land in Africa, but being Africans themselves have a heart for the continent. In another example, displaced Zimbabwean farmers were absorbed by the Nigerian government and allocated huge amounts of land. These farmers are said to have turned around the face of agriculture and boosted food production in Nigeria.

What we are seeing is definitely answers to prayer and prophecy, and can be a blessing to the continent and those who embark on agriculture ventures.

Biofuels

Biofuels offer another potential agriculture opportunity. Demand is increasing. For example, the European Union had a policy target that 18 metric tons of biofuels should be used by the transport sector by 2010, when in 2006 use was only 2 metric tons.

Currently, many people argue against the use of edible foods for the production of biofuels as this drives up the cost of food. However, researchers are discovering new plants, such as the jatropha tree, which is able to produce biofuels in significant quantity yet is not an edible food.

Jatropha is already successfully being grown in large quantities in India, and is the fuel used to power trains. An added advantage is the ability of this plant to grow in arid areas and wastelands.

Africa has large swathes of desert areas and wastelands. This is a waiting investment opportunity. It also offers positive environmental impact as these trees would help to stem desert encroachment.

Jatropha can also be planted on other arable land and, while the trees are growing, this land can be used for the growing of food crops. Jatropha trees, in this case, provide shade for other crops.

Environmentalists favor mixed farming like this against monocultures. On the other hand, research and development regarding fertilizers, plant diseases, appropriate biocides, and the best way to grow Jatropha is still in the early stages.

Palm Oil

In another example, China signed a contract with the DRC to produce palm oil for biofuels on 2.8 million hectares of land. The global demand for palm oil is expected to rise and double by 2020, according to TransGraph Consulting.

The demand for palm oil is not just for biofuels, but for cooking oil and other applications. China is currently one of the largest potential consumer markets for palm oil exports from Africa since palm oil is not produced in China. China has the world's largest consumer market at this time and they have a growing number of preferential trade agreements with African countries. If a foreign investor develops palm oil plantations and processing facilities in Africa along with local partners, he or she can also find favorable paths to export to other high demand markets like China.

While Asia is the key market for palm oil, the consumption of palm oil in the U.S. is also rising. The FDA requirement for companies to list partially hydrogenated oils on labels is driving companies to find alternatives, which includes palm oil.

Palms grow in abundance in West and Central Africa. In fact, the palms grown in Malaysia originated in West Africa. Because palms grow in abundance, they are used for cooking oil and other applications in local markets, so palms are a natural asset to leverage for production, local sales, and exports.

Palm oil is becoming big business in Africa with companies like Sime Darby, one of the largest crude palm oil producers in the world, establishing plantations in Africa. Malaysia-based Sime Darby signed an agreement with the Liberian government to cultivate 220,000 hectares for palm and rubber in 2010.

There are concerns over how people and the environment will fare as demand increases for palm oil. But some non-profits have shaped strategies to benefit both. All for Africa (www.allforafrica.org) developed a project called "Palm Out of Poverty," which will benefit both local economies and be environmentally sustainable.

Government Investment in Africa

More African governments are discovering the potential of agriculture and investing in food production as a means to economic development. Agriculture is seen as having a far greater potential to create jobs than any other sector, and thus a means to alleviate poverty.

Through the African Union New Economic Partnership for African Development (NEPAD) initiative, African governments decided to commit 10% of their national budgets to agriculture. This means good news for investors because more public funding is being channeled into solving the basic shortages in infrastructure, research, and other inputs.

Not only will this increase governmental focus on agricultural productivity, but offers business opportunities to foreign companies to come with technological solutions, which they can sell to government and private sector. At the 2010 African Growth Opportunity Act (AGOA) conference in the United States, that is precisely what the U.S. government promoted to agricultural producers. In addition, U.S. companies through their African partners can export into the U.S. with preferential status through AGOA.

Already, some of these investments have brought about visible solutions and success stories. In Mozambique, for instance, "virtual knowledge centers" are being created to link the country's farm scientists to rural communities and direct researchers to identify problems and create solutions. In another instance, Nigeria, Niger, and Uganda have brought together research institutes, extension agents, and farmers' organizations to introduce improved crop varieties of staples.

In Uganda, farmers are growing NERICA rice varieties in upland areas that had never produced rice before. Uganda is now a net exporter of rice.

Malawi is another success story after significant government investment in agriculture. Its success story stunned donors. In 2005, the nation's leadership, tired of going to beg for foreign aid, found ways to empower local farmers through the launching of a fertilizer subsidy project. This subsidy reduced a 50 kilogram bag of fertilizer from about $27 to $6.50. As a result, maize production jumped from 1.2 million metric tons in 2005 to 2.7 million metric tons in 2006 and 3.4 million metric tons in 2007, creating a surplus of 1.5 million metric tons.

The better harvest did not just benefit Malawi, but also its neighboring countries. According to the USAID-funded Famine Early Warning System Network, Malawi officially exported 286,589 tons of maize to Zimbabwe by the end of December 2007. Also, the World Food Programme (WFP) sent 32,363 tons of Malawian maize to Zimbabwe, bringing total official exports from Malawi to Zimbabwe to 321,406 tons that year.

Not only did this success make Malawian farmers richer, it went a long way to prove the potential of agriculture within the continent.

Tackling Challenges of Agriculture in Africa While Creating Opportunities

Some of the challenges faced by the agricultural sector in Africa are inadequate infrastructure, e.g., roads, electricity; shortage of inputs like seeds and fertilizer; limited access to equipment and machinery for large scale farming; and land ownership issues. Every one of these challenges offers investment opportunity.

In the Naivasha district of Kenya, for instance, the challenge of bad road infrastructure adversely affected rose growers. Competing growers got together and fixed up their roads, thereby supporting the industry.[29] The horticulture industry is Kenya's top foreign exchange earner, making $922 million in 2009. Kenya exports 1,000 tons of produce and flowers, including roses, carnations, and lilies, per day. This sub-sector employs 50,000-70,000 people directly and over 1.5 million people indirectly.

Another solution, which is systematic, is agriculture growth corridors. They are development corridors focused on the entire agricultural value chain from growing to harvesting to transporting to exporting. They are seen as a means to catalyze both agricultural and economic development. They generally follow the development of existing transport corridors, e.g., Harare-Mutare-Beira.

In Africa, private sector, government, and NGOs collaborate on such initiatives. Yara International, one of the biggest fertilizer producers globally, and the African Green Revolution Forum (AGRF) are spearheading two agricultural growth corridors – Beira covering Mozambique, Malawi, and Zimbabwe, and Southern covering Tanzania, Malawi, Zambia, and the DRC.

NEPAD has thrown its support into the concept of leveraging the improvements expected along 12 development corridors in Africa for agriculture. They have set up a separate organization called TransFarm Africa (TFA) to spearhead the initiative. Among its initiatives is an enterprise investment fund for agriculture called TFA Transformation Fund.

As these develop, expect opportunities to grow like along transport corridors connecting major cities along the coast and in the interior of Africa. If foreign investors or businesses partner with local

---

[29] Vos Iz Neias. (April 20, 2010). Nairobi, Kenya – Effect of Volcanic Ash: 10 Million Roses Ruined. Accessed online at http://www.vosizneias.com/53650/2010/04/20/nairobi-kenya-effect-of-volcanic-ash-10-million-roses-ruined (January 11, 2011).

African agricultural firms, they will be able to leverage more of the benefits from these initiatives.

With Africa's natural assets conducive to agriculture and the increasing demand for food globally, Africa is headed down the path of being the key breadbasket for the world, if developed correctly.

This offers extraordinary opportunities for businesses and investors for a long time.

Information Communication Technologies (ICT)

The last decade saw a tremendous boom in ICT in Africa. The key sector is mobile, which continues to grow at astronomical rates. From virtually no mobile phone users in 1999, mobile phone users in Africa will reach 500 million soon. Africa may have double the number of mobile phone users than in the United States within a few years.

In fact, according to the International Telecommunications Union (ITU)[30], Africa is the fastest growing mobile market. In 2010, ITU said that Africa's mobile user growth rate has exceeded 60% annually for the five previous years, double the global average. Africa is in fact the first continent where mobile subscribers outstrip fixed-line users.

This is an example how Africa has and can leapfrog the slow development cycle. The story behind the mobile market is that the fixed-line market was controlled by state-owned enterprises, which were inefficient and slow to develop infrastructure. Service was also expensive because of a lack of competition.

Companies like Vodacom in South Africa sought mobile licenses instead since state-owned institutions did not operate in this realm. In addition, it was much quicker to deploy mobile phone infrastructure. And, the mobile phone operators found solutions,

---

[30] http://www.itu.int

such as prepaid services and SMS, so that most people, from poor to rich, could access and use mobile phones.

In the mobile space, Africa leads Western markets with innovative solutions like SMS-based applications and prepaid services. For example, Ushahidi is a web/SMS integrated solution which allows anyone to report critical incident information. It evolved from a request by Ory Okolloh, a Kenyan blogger and former corporate affairs officer for Enablis in South Africa, for any developer who could help her develop a platform so that people could report on incidents in the violence following the Kenyan 2007 elections. The application was developed within a few days. It was also used to report Haiti relief efforts by disaster agencies and track issues and tips in the snow storm coined "Snowmageddon" in Washington, DC in 2010.

Mobile payments and banking have taken off in Kenya with M-Pesa and M-Kesho. Out of a population of close to 40 million, estimates are that 38% of adult users have M-PESA accounts and that over 7.7 million accounts had been registered as of August 2009, according to the report, *The Economics of M-Pesa.*[31]

High-Speed Broadband Boom

Broadband is estimated to contribute 1.3% to economic growth for every 10% jump in availability, according to the World Bank. Unfortunately, this is one area that Africa continued to lag behind Western countries. Only a few years ago, Africa as a whole had less than one terabit/second capacity. This is dramatically changing with the continent's connection to international bandwidth expected to reach over 20 terabits/second within the next few years. The following

---

[31] Jack, W., & Suri, T. (2010). The Economics of M-Pesa. Accessed online at http://www.mit.edu/~tavneet/M-PESA.pdf (January 6, 2011).

image shows the major fiber connections, including projections through 2012.

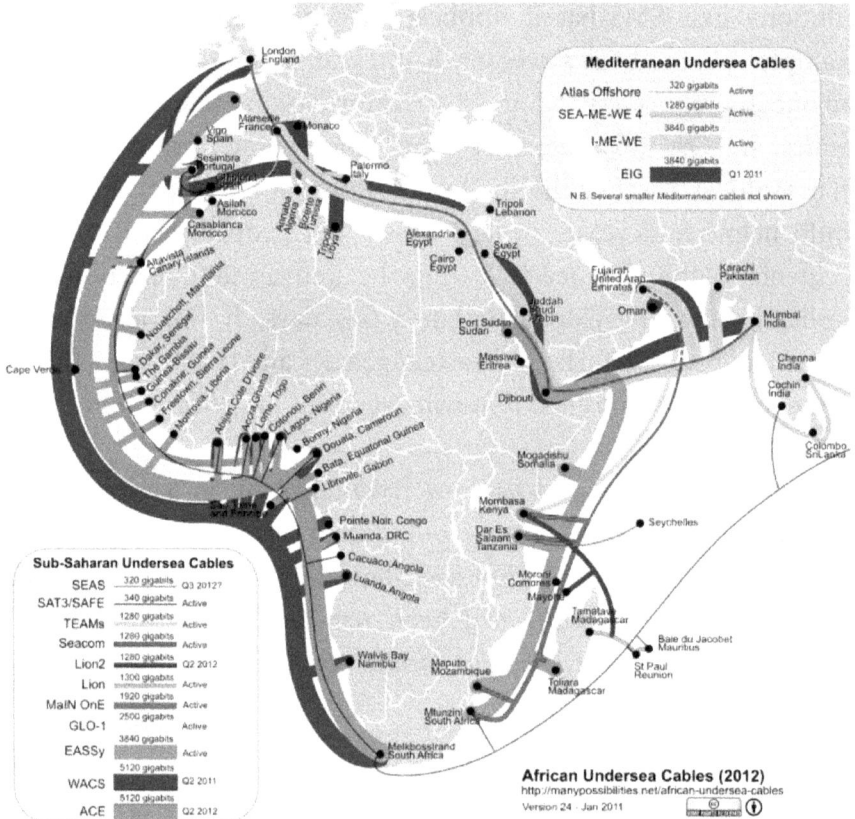

Source: Manypossibilities.net

Countries along the coast of Africa, where the cables land, get the most immediate benefit due to their proximity. Kenya is a prime example. Kenya's ICT sector was actually waiting like a racehorse in the starting gate for the cable to land and be switched on.

One priority sub-sector in Kenya that benefits greatly from the new bandwidth is business process outsourcing (BPO). Beyond the fact that labor is cheaper, Kenyans speak English well and are better educated in general than other regions of Sub-Saharan Africa. So, Kenya can likely establish competitive advantage in this space, but they were losing their advantage because the cost of ICT infrastructure was three to four times their competitors. When SEACOM landed in 2009, costs dropped and Internet use climbed even though it is still low compared to Western standards.

One differing variable in broadband users in the West and Africa is that the uptake on the Internet is expected to be primarily from mobile devices instead of computers because of cost and the broad population's comfort with mobile devices compared to computers.

There are still two key challenges for the broadband market – backhaul and access. Backhaul is the land-based fiber optic cable lines. Major countries, such as Nigeria, South Africa, and Kenya, have worked on this to cover at least the major markets in the country. East Africa did well as a region by connecting major areas throughout each country in the East Africa Community – Burundi, Kenya, Rwanda, Tanzania, and Uganda – and between each country, so the foundation to connect a common market of over 140 million people is there. There is progress with backhaul all over Africa.[32]

As an alternative, and to cover areas not easily reached by fiber, is the O3B Networks satellite solution, which will provide affordable broadband anywhere in Africa. They will be fully live in 2012.

The third leg of broadband infrastructure and the toughest challenge is access. This is where people are provided the services and equipment to use the Internet. The number of people with both computers and Internet access in Africa is extremely low. In 2008, there were only four African countries in which close to or over 10% of the households had both a computer and Internet access. Two of

---

[32] Visit http://www.afribiz.net/insightareas/information-communication-technologies for more details.

the countries are in North Africa and the other two are island nations in Southern Africa. (See the table below.)

Country	Has Computer	Has Internet Access
Mauritius	19.1%	20.2%
Morocco	10.0%	13.7%
Seychelles	10.0%	13.0%
Egypt	9.5%	12.9%

Source: International Telecommunications Union (ITU)

Governments, non-profits, and private sector are working to provide access in community labs, internet cafes, schools, and even mobile labs to rural areas. My (Lauri's) company was a subcontractor at one point on a project, which placed a computer lab with Internet access in over 2,000 schools in Gauteng province, South Africa. While the project had a lot of challenges and changes in regime, it finally got the infrastructure in place in 2010 after over five years since its original inception.

When I visited Egypt in 2004, I was excited to see that they had ADSL technology to connect to the Internet at decent speeds, but this was not a typical scenario for the rest of Africa. Some other countries like South Africa introduced ADSL. However, this technology is based on copper wire technology, so it didn't become pervasive because Africa lacked copper wire infrastructure, considering fixed-line infrastructure was, and still is, weak.

Hence, wireless has become the promising channel to deliver broadband to users. Wireless technologies include the external infrastructure, such as metropolitan area networks, and devices, such as mobile phones and data cards. In fact, 4G technology was implemented in South Africa before it was implemented in the

United States. This dynamic may change some with external infrastructure as fiber optic backhaul is rolled out.

Opportunities in ICT in Africa

To contextualize the opportunities in ICT in Africa, think of two major occurrences in the United States. First, there was the break-up of AT&T in the mid-80s. Second, there is Internet infrastructure development, which has risen since the 1990s. This is where Africa is headed, just leaving the starting gate.

Opportunities in ICT present themselves in the ICT sector, as well as a supporting sector of other sectors. First, in the ICT sector there are still pockets of opportunities for basic infrastructure, but by and large those opportunities go to very large companies and consortia. However, thinking about the boom of Internet and telecommunications in the United States, you can imagine the millions of opportunities to provide products and services.

Second, computer and mobile phone equipment and accessories with configurations that will suit the African consumer and at prices they can afford is another opportunity. The college student market in Nigeria is a prime example. This large youth population has disposable income and sees the mobile phone and computer as essentials, according to Nwakego Eyisi, founder of Encompass Analytics of Nigeria, economist, and an Afribiz Media featured columnist. Nissi, one of the authors, has also found a market for netbooks because of the lower cost and many consumers do not necessarily need the processing power of full laptops in African markets.

Third, there are still many opportunities for providing training and consulting services, particularly if you are able to work with local partners. But the biggest opportunities, and the fourth area of opportunity, are in developing mobile, SMS, and Internet applications, as well as content, for the local markets.

One of the remaining critical challenges with the school lab project I mentioned earlier is the development of local content. This is echoed throughout Africa. In an interview with Guy Zibi, CEO of AfricaNext Research, he indicated that local content development is indeed a big potential market.

As a sign of the coming growing content market, Limelight Networks, which is a content delivery platform in the United States, partnered with Business Connexion of South Africa. This partnership will provide the platform and content on it to African markets, starting with South Africa, as well as provide African content to the world.

From a segment perspective, expect to find growth in mobile worker and home-based business segments. This will likely take flight in economic hubs, which have strong intellectual and knowledge-based economies, such as South Africa. Lucienne Abrahams and Mark Burke, researchers at the LINKS Centre at WITS University in Johannesburg, suggest that the unit of production in South Africa will shift back to the home from the office, or centralized workplaces, and that the government should actually focus resources to support this trend believing they will get better return on investment concerning economic development.

Another segment for ICT is users of smart phones. The market for smart phones is expected to grow by 50% and represents almost one in five handsets sold in Africa in 2011, according to International Data Corporation (IDC).

It is likely that South Africa will represent one of the key smart phone markets as it demonstrated strong growth in 2009 and 2010, even during the economic crisis. But the smart phone market will also grow well in urban, economic hubs like capital cities and regional economic hubs – Kenya, Nigeria, Egypt, and South Africa. You can also look to segments of business like multinationals whose personnel likely possess smart phones for work.

Another way to focus on opportunities is by sector. For instance, travel services over mobiles is a growing sub-sector globally and since the mobile, including smart phone, market is growing well in Africa, it has potential in Africa particularly if you can provide local content.

Another instance is mobile learning. A priority social sector for African countries is education. In most countries, the administration, facilities, and number of professionals needed are lacking to meet demand. Closing the gap is not a short-term effort, it could take several decades. However, mobile phones with broadband to provide access to the Internet can present an entirely different scenario.

And finally, ICT is transforming agriculture in Africa. The Ethiopian Commodities Exchange (ECX) is a world-class, technology-driven exchange making Ethiopian agricultural products available globally. It's amazing this could happen in a country where household ownership of computers and access to the Internet is below 1%.

There are a myriad of innovations and opportunities in Africa for those in the technology sector and those outside of the industry.[33] The key is to focus on those technologies and opportunities that you can understand and use your strengths.

Conclusion

In this chapter, we only covered three streams of opportunities in Africa, but within each of the streams you can see multitudes of opportunities. If you are new to Africa, you will likely get overwhelmed with the sheer volume of opportunities. It causes

---

33 For more information on opportunities in the ICT market in Africa, visit http://www.afribiz.net/insightareas/information-communication-technologies.

people to find it hard to focus, but it presents an excellent opportunity for you to be led by the Holy Spirit.

The next two chapters will delve more deeply into two specific opportunities – gold and consumer markets. If your mind thought of Africa as a place of poverty and not a place to explore business opportunities, and it has not shifted somewhat in the other direction after these chapters, we haven't done our job well enough. But don't take our word for it, confirm with the Lord.

4

Gold'en' Opportunities in Africa

Hartmut Sieper

This chapter is about investments - good investments.

We are living in a world that has experienced major paradigm shifts within a very short period of time, and will continue to do so. Some of them are already recognized by many people, others are not. The most powerful developments that are about to unfold are invisible for the majority of people.

We have to put our discussion about doing business and making investments in Africa into a global context. We need to draw a big picture in order to fully understand the strong underlying forces that shape the world of tomorrow.

There is an increasing polarity in many aspects. We have to define our position and find our way between the following antipodes:

- financial assets (e.g., fixed time deposits, bonds, bond funds, foreign exchange) versus hard assets (e.g., commodities, real estate, land)
- developed world versus developing world
- savings attitude versus debt attitude
- freedom versus control
- and finally the world versus the Kingdom

The Principle of Sowing and Harvesting

When talking about investment, we have to think about behavioral patterns of spending money and private consumption. Avoid the "buy now and pay later" attitude. Stay away from debt as much as you can. Debt will hold you in bondage. According to the Bible, debtors are slaves to their creditors: "The rich rule over the poor, and the borrower is servant to the lender." (New International Version, Proverbs 22:7). As this becomes increasingly true when the overall economic situation gets worse, you should try to get out of debt as fast as possible. In many cases, this would mean to consume much less than you have been accustomed to.

Even when you are debt free, investment is better than consumption. Investing means you are getting ready for the future while consumption stands for immediate satisfaction of needs. Postponed needs will allow you to save money in the present, which might lead to a more prosperous future. First, you have to save, and then you can invest. The opposing force of the Wealth spirit is the Debt spirit.

The Bible tells us a lot about the principle of sowing and harvesting. First you have to sow, and then you wait for the harvest. Farmers have to do a lot of work in the sowing season. They have to prepare the fields. Then, they sow the seeds and cover it with the fertile soil. Within the growing season, they have to water the plants and remove weeds. During the ripening season, the farmer can be more relaxed and just watch the fruits mature. In the harvesting season, again a lot of work has to be done which is very different from the work during the other seasons. Finally, the produce will be sold on the market, which will give the farmer the financial return of his enterprise, and some will be stored for the future.

When you are doing private equity investments, the processes can be compared with the work of farmers. Before you invest, you have to examine the soil (project), select the right field (market), purchase the appropriate seed (product, business model), and assign the right farmer (manager, staff).

When you invest, you have to keep an eye on the water (financials) and protect your crop (business) against weeds and vermin (competitors). When the crop grows (the business model works), you can accumulate wealth step by step and see the fruit ripening (the balance sheet growing and profits increasing). Finally, the harvesting season stands for cashing in on the investment. When you deliver the produce to the market (sell the business), you will know that you have done very well.

Some additional points must be made. Good farmers avoid selecting the wrong seed or sowing it into ground of unknown quality. They also want to be sure about the potential market for the fruit to be grown. This means for potential investors, "Do not buy into something which you do not fully understand." Smart investors follow the rule "If you doubt, stay out".

Another investment rule is "BLASH". What does it mean? "BLASH" is the abbreviation for "Buy Low and Sell High". It is not as easy as it sounds, because nobody can tell you which price is high and which is low. This is especially true for the stock markets.

When talking about taking advantage of business opportunities in Africa, smart investors should comply with this rule. If you want to buy property, it should be more advantageous in the long term to purchase land or real estate in places that are not yet in favor of the big money. Right now, prices are very high in cities like Luanda, Douala, and Dakar. The capital city of Angola is one of the most expensive cities in the world. In contrast, Harare is still cheap. If I would have to choose, I would rather invest in Zimbabwe[34] than in Angola, at least from an anti-cyclical point of view.

Wise and Foolish Governments

Unfortunately, very few governments of nations follow honest investment rules. Most presidents, ministers, authorities, and ruling political parties are more geared towards being re-elected, or staying in power, than doing the right things in the right way. So, they court voters and give them presents by spending more money than they earn. This is the basic reason for deficit spending.

From a Kingdom perspective, the Keynesian approach of deficit spending in economic downturns is a wrong strategy. In Genesis 41, the Bible tells us a different way. Pharaoh's dream about the seven good cows and good ears of corn, and subsequently the seven lean cows and worthless ears of corn is a warning. In this parable, God is telling us to accumulate wealth in good years, because you will need to have resources in bad years. Or, to put it another way, "Save now, then you will have in cases of need."

Wise rulers save money in prosperous years in order to have a financial cushion, which will help them to survive in bad years. Finance ministers of wise governments use the trade surplus of prosperous years to reduce sovereign debt instead of following the temptation of spending more money in order to please voters. This was the case with Nigeria from the oil revenues they gained when crude oil prices rose rapidly, so when the economic crisis occurred the country had cash to weather the storm.

---

[34] People assume that because there are economic sanctions on Zimbabwe's President Robert Mugabe and those associated with him that Western businesses cannot do business in Zimbabwe. That's not true. For United States investors and businesses, there are certain sanctions, but you can do business in Zimbabwe. Check with the U.S. State Department or the U.S. embassy in Zimbabwe for further details.

Only in bad years do wise governments borrow money from their people and foreign investors. The unpleasant reality is that regular sovereign debt retirement is not on the agenda of most governments. Foolish governments pile up debt in good years and in bad years, although at different speeds. The task for paying back the debt is left for our children and grandchildren.

But wait a minute, this is about to change. More and more people understand that coming out of the financial calamities of today can no longer be delegated to the next generation. It is our generation that will have to pay the price. As believers, we should leave the Babylonian system as fast as we can. Ask the Lord to guide you in this process.

Thank God, not all governments have been acting foolishly. There are a few exceptions. Norway has used its abundant wealth of mineral oil by putting money into a sovereign wealth fund which is the second biggest in the world, after the one operated by Abu Dhabi. The Norwegians decided not to join the European Union, which was a wise decision. So, they will be able to use the accumulated wealth for their own people. The Norwegians will not be forced to support other nations, who acted unwisely, financially.

One year after independence, the big diamond resources of Botswana were discovered. Botswana, which was one of the poorest nations in the world in those days, used the proceeds from diamond exports to sustainably develop the country, and the ruling politicians have resisted the temptation of misusing the nation's wealth for their private vaults. As a result, Botswana became one of the fastest growing nations in the world. If more African nations followed the role model of Botswana, the continent would grow even faster and would be able to solve more problems in the short time than it is doing now.

The good news is that more and more African nations are aware of the need for sustainable economic development, which includes social and environmental aspects. Ghana, for example, wants to wisely use the newly found richness of mineral oil reserves by avoiding the apparent mistakes that Nigeria has made over the last two decades. Nigeria focused too much on crude oil and disregarded the rest of the economy and thereby became ill with the Dutch disease. To master these challenges is one of the biggest tasks of African nations with abundant wealth of mineral resources.

However, I am very positive that most African nations will finally succeed in unleashing an amount of wealth that will transcend the proceeds from export of crude oil, copper, gold, platinum, coal, and other primary resources.

The Future of the Euro

In contrast to Norway, Germany is bound in the European Union. The strongest economy in Europe quickly becomes the lender of last resort to failing Southern and Western European nations, namely Greece, Ireland, and Portugal, possibly followed by Spain and eventually by Italy, Austria, and Belgium as well. These countries are financially weak, partly because of high sovereign debt and partly because of overleveraged banking systems.

I can see very clearly that the financial systems in Europe are not sustainable. There is no simple way out. The financial mechanisms of avoiding, or rather postponing, the final collapse are highly unrighteous. Countries like Greece and Portugal, that are no longer competitive, do not have the choice to devalue their currencies, as they have done in former decades because they are members of the Euro zone. They have only two alternatives: they can reduce their cost of production by 30% which would mean that all salaries and pensions would have to be drastically cut, and therefore regain competitiveness, or they will need ongoing transfer payments from the richer countries.

As political correctness does not allow policymakers to challenge the Euro (all heads of state are continuously arguing that the Euro is "without alternative"), the downward spiral towards a transfer union is predetermined. However, this transfer union cannot solve the problems, which are caused by underlying iniquities and a perverted mixture of governments making deficits, central banks printing money, and financial institutions speculating rather than doing honest business.

As a result of that, hard-working German taxpayers have to send their money to Greek magistrates that are allowed to retire at age 50, receiving 100% of their latest paycheck. In the long term, these developments will create social unrest. It might take some years before European citizens will behave like the people of Tunisia in January 2011, but the risk of social upheaval in the Western world, including the United States and the United Kingdom, is clearly on the rise.

Note: *I think that the riots in Tunisia, having forced the former president Ben Ali to flee out of the country, is God's answer to many prayers against corrupt leaders, arbitrary acts by the authorities, and Heads of State that are using their political power for personal enrichment rather than leading their country and society into a better future. The turmoil in Tunisia is also a sign that the people of a suffering country are willing to fight for democracy and good governance. In the long term, the development towards democracy in Africa will be strengthened, thus reducing political and economic risk for investors and entrepreneurs.*

At this time, we are also seeing an escalation of protests in Egypt. If Egypt's government is ousted or transforms, this will likely create a major domino effect in the Middle East.

From my point of view, there are strong arguments for the assumption that the Euro will finally break. It is just a matter of time. The countries of the Euro zone in Northern and Southern Europe, as well as in Western and Eastern Europe, are too different from each other - in cultural as well as in economic terms - to put them under one currency roof. Before the Euro was established in 2002, the countries could balance out their different economic power, development speed, and competitiveness by re-evaluating or devaluating their national currencies.

The differences between countries like Germany and Greece are so huge that they cannot remain under the same currency roof for a long time. This is simply not possible. Critics of the Euro have pinpointed to this inbuilt weakness right from the beginning. They still think and argue that the end of the Euro would be the "best" for Germany, as well as for Greece. We all know that there are no good choices at all. There are only bad solutions, but some are less painful than others.

However, this thinking is against political correctness in Europe, and no mainstream media channels are reporting this. Last year, there was a big investment conference on "The End of the Euro" in Berlin, the capital city of Germany, with more than 700 people attending. Despite sincere marketing efforts and press releases from the organizers of this conference, no journalists from the print media or TV stations showed up. This remarkable event was completely neglected by German newspapers, business magazines, and TV channels. The only media that reported in detail was a Russian broadcast network.

I believe that this is a clear sign that freedom in Europe is threatened. Right now, the Hungarian government wants to abolish the freedom of the press in Hungary. Nowadays, you can be sentenced in one member country of the European Union if you commit a crime according to the rule of law of any other member country, even if this is not a crime in your home country. The vast majority of Europeans do not understand what is really going on, and what is being prepared behind the scene. The overall picture is frightening.

In Europe, the long-term trend towards further integration will probably discontinue. Although politicians from all countries and parties continuously stress that Europe is still moving into the direction of increasing political, economic, judicial, and tax unity, the precarious financial situation of countries like Greece, Ireland, Portugal, the United Kingdom, and maybe others points to another direction.

The New World of Investing

Whether we like it or not, we have to accept that the economic power is shifting from the United States and Europe to Asia and the emerging markets. Investors and business people that want to prosper have to adjust themselves to these new trends and to look for opportunities in growth regions. This shift will allow each country to thrive in its own competitive space as God has designed.

The "investment train" is already on its way. It will stop at a few more railway stations, and some more passengers will have the opportunity to board the train. Those who are hesitating will be left behind on the platform when the doors close and the train leaves the station. As the speed of the train increases, it will become more difficult and dangerous to jump onto the "investment" cars. At some time in the future, it will not be possible any longer.

What does this allegory mean in the context of finances? I can see the real danger that citizens of debt loaded countries of the developed world will have a limited window of opportunity to put their capital into promising investments and ventures in countries outside their home country.

The background of this consideration is the possibility of new foreign exchange and capital transfer controls that might be imposed by the governments of financially failing nations. As soon as such controls are established, it might become either very expensive or even impossible for companies and private individuals to command where their money goes. This was happening in the hyperinflation period in Zimbabwe in 2008 and 2009, when the Zimbabwean stock market was the only avenue to escape from rapid devaluation of the local currency. During the financial crisis of Argentina, exchange controls made it impossible for locals to get out of their Pesos.

Wherever and whenever a nation's currency was in acute danger, governments have imposed exchange controls as a desperate attempt to defend the currency. In most cases, it didn't work out and the financial outcome of those people who missed the train was just disastrous.

Debt, Inflation, and the Printing Machine

Let us complete the big picture by stressing the fact that central banks all over the world are accelerating the printing of money, or a better way of saying it is, creating it electronically out of thin air. The U.S. Federal Reserve has to print money because investors from overseas no longer subscribe to U.S. Treasury Bonds. T-Bonds that are due have to be financed by the printing press.

Every intelligent person will easily understand that this is not a solution. Paying back debt by accumulating more debt is a vicious circle that inevitably will lead to the destruction of the national currency and the national wealth. The sovereign credit rating agencies like Standard & Poor's have been threatening again to reduce the U.S. credit rating, if the debt is not brought lower, which means it will cost more to borrow in the future. This process, however, will take a while.

The key question that is being asked by many market participants is whether deflation or inflation will be revealed as the main destructive force. However, at the end, the results will be the same. In former centuries, nations with huge debt, which they could not pay back, ended in default or inflation. For politicians, inflation is the better choice.

Hence, it follows that an inflationary environment is highly probable for the U.S. and Europe. I even think that a hyperinflation scenario for the United States is not out of range.

At some point, the deterioration of the financial situation of overleveraged banks and failing states will quickly accelerate and lead to sudden bad surprises. This will happen when trust disappears.

Our financial systems are based on trust. There is no tangible backing of national currencies. Most Western banks have no real substance because their balance sheets that have become non-transparent since the latest changes of accounting standards are overloaded with toxic securities of little or no value.

Only a few depositors are aware of this, and most of them are still maintaining their bank accounts, because they trust in the banking system and the reliability of deposit protection schemes. Additionally, leading politicians have assured depositors that governments would guarantee the deposits.

The systemic banks have been declared too big to fail - so far so good. The pivotal point is that the time will come when financial institutions will become too big to bail.

This was the case in Iceland in 2008. The big Icelandic banks could not be rescued by the government because the amount of money needed was too huge, amounting to 10 times GDP. Iceland was the first state default in the financial crisis. The collapsing Irish banks were too big for the Irish government to bail them out, so the whole country had to be rescued by the European Union. If Austrian banks would fail because they have massively invested into Eastern Europe, Austria would not be able to bail them out. In this case, the country of Austria would have to be rescued financially.

So far, small countries have been hit. What will happen if big countries fail? What will happen when there is no more last resort? When trust is no longer there, how can a system, which is based on trust, continue to function? This is food for thought.

Good and Bad Investment Rules

It is of utmost importance for Kingdom-minded people to act very wisely and proactively in order to miss the invisible traps that are lying in front of us. Scripture says, "The prudent see danger and take refuge, but the simple keep going and suffer for it." (New International Version, Proverbs 27:12).

The following choices are good investments for storing and accumulating wealth:

- Precious metals (physical bars and coins, NOT paper gold). Please note Exchange Traded Funds (ETFs) are paper gold. If confiscation of gold should occur, Uncle Sam would most probably start at GLD and other ETFs.
- Real estate for own housing. Debt-free real estate can be considered as hard assets while real estate purchased against credit has to be seen as a financial asset due to the dependency on paying interest and paying back the loan.
- Stocks that are cheap and pay good dividends. On African stock markets, there are many stocks which pay reliable dividends that incur very high, sometimes double-digit dividend yields. I have allocated some of those stocks into the pan-African mutual fund that I am advising.

- Participation in solid SMMEs with good business models. I think this should be the preferred option among the body of Christ in the end times. If Christian entrepreneurs and Kingdom companies are financed by private equity investments from Christian investors, they step out of the Babylonian system.

All these investments can be considered as a hedge against a major currency crisis. On the other hand, there are some bad investments that you should avoid:

- Fixed income securities of highly indebted municipalities (i.e., municipal bonds) and sovereign nations (i.e., U.S. Treasury Bonds). You might not get your money back when the debt instrument is due.
- Bonds from financially weak companies. They might not be able to pay back the loan.
- Highly leveraged financial instruments. You not only have the risk of losing money very quickly because of the high leverage, there is also the counterparty risk, which would apply in the case of a collapsing market.
- Too much money in bank accounts and fixed term deposits, since those liquid instruments might be in acute danger when the next boost in the global banking crisis comes. Do not trust in "insurances" like the Federal Deposit Insurance Corporation (FDIC) because their capacities for bailing out failing banks are limited.
- Fairly valued and overvalued stocks.

Gold as an Investment

Gold seems to be one of the key investments in the world of today and tomorrow. In Biblical times, gold, silver, seed, and flour, were all used as money (Leviticus 27:16, 2 Kings 7:1). The vast majority of times when gold and silver are mentioned in the Bible, it is in reference to the wealth of the kings of Israel or to the wealth of the temple of the Lord. Additionally, gold and silver were used in the workings and furnishings of the Ark of the Covenant, as well as the vessels in the temple.

Gold and silver are truly the only Biblically-approved forms of money according to Hebrew law, and the metals are the very embodiment of "just weights and measures." The Bible calls unjust weights and measures as "an abomination to the Lord" (Leviticus 19:35, Deuteronomy 25:15, Proverbs 20:10). Therefore, gold is definitely approved by God for men to use as money and as a store of wealth.

But gold means more than that. By owning the yellow metal in physical form as bars and coins, you truly get out of Babylon. Why is that so? There are no liabilities of third parties attached to bullion gold while paper money is just a piece of paper with the promise of a central bank written on it.

What kind of promise are we actually trusting when we deal with U.S. Dollars? In fact, there is no real promise. On the U.S. Dollar note, it is mentioned "This Note Is Legal Tender For All Debts Public And Private." There is no longer a statement about the right to exchange dollars for gold. Until 1913, U.S. Dollars could be converted into gold coins to the bearer on demand. What a difference! A century ago, most currencies were backed by gold, directly or indirectly. Nowadays, all currencies in the world are pure paper currencies, without tangible assets as backing. In fact, it is against the rules of the International Monetary Fund to back a currency with physical assets.

However, there is an interesting new development in the United States. In some regions, precious metal coins have been circulated. Some politicians want U.S. states to introduce gold and silver coins as legal tender, referring to the U.S. Constitution.

Now take a look at the huge debt of most of our Western economies, many companies, and most private households. Indebted private individuals, legal entities, cities, counties, states, and nations are slaves to the lenders. The lenders are owners of treasury bonds, municipal bonds, and collaterals of debtors. What will happen if the debtors fail to pay interest or even to pay back the debt?

The reality is most indebted Western economies will never pay back their debt. The United States would not be able to do that even if the income tax rate was 100%. The point of no return already passed many years ago. The interesting fact is that many holders of U.S. Treasury Bonds are aware of that. So what they have is a piece of paper with a promise that most probably will not be fulfilled.

The financial system, and all investments of pension funds, insurance companies, mutual funds, etc., is based on interest. Many market participants are feeling increasingly unwell, but they trust on their ability to get out of the endangered financial instruments, if they have to. This is a very dangerous way of thinking. If a horde of elephants wants to trample through a narrow door, there is no way out. So, what options do we have?

Gold represents a value in itself. It is a rare chemical element that cannot be produced out of other elements. It is not connected to any paper currency. There are no liabilities of promises of third parties attached to it. Gold is being traded all over the world.

The possession of bullion gold was forbidden for U.S. citizens from 1934 to 1971. It cannot be ruled out that having or buying gold may become illegal again. From my point of view, this threat is biggest in the U.S., followed by the European Union. Countries like Switzerland, which is not a part of the EU, Dubai, Singapore, Hong Kong and Panama, are much more secure places.

I don't think that there will be any restrictions on gold ownership and trading. If you are a U.S. citizen, you might consider participating in a gold mining company instead of owning gold. Africa is full of promising opportunities.

Gold'en' Opportunities in Africa

Let us come back to the spiritual importance of gold as a means for wealth preservation. While metals like copper, platinum, and chromium are used in industry and therefore exposed to economic cycles, which might become a problem in a recession or depression of the Western economies, gold is different. If you understand gold as the ultimate currency, then the basic business model of a gold mining company is virtually producing money. So, it might be a good idea to have ownership in a gold mine somewhere in Africa, far away from any Western jurisdictions.

During intense research on that topic, I found out that there is an interesting market niche in small-scale mining in countries like Ghana, Zimbabwe, Tanzania, the DRC, and other countries with alluvial gold deposits. Many of those deposits are small in size but have high grades. They are too small for the big mining companies like AngloGold Ashanti, BHP Billiton, and Rio Tinto; hence there is very little competition. Alluvial deposits along current and ancient rivers are shallow, have thin overburden, and can be mined easily with some low-tech equipment.

You only need a prospecting or mining license, some capital for purchasing the equipment and hiring people, some knowledge about the processes, diesel supply for power generation, and a water source on the ground. Basic equipment includes a bulldozer for earth movements, a stone crusher, a separator, a pump with a water pipe, and maybe a mining shaft. Then, you can start.

Last year, I visited some small-scale mining operations in the Greenbelt zone of Zimbabwe, where there are a lot of artisanal gold miners. Most of them do not have enough capital for buying machines. They take the ore out of the ground with very basic means and bring the ore to a better equipped gold mine to process it.

A mechanical separator can get approximately 1/2 of the gold out of the stones. For this work, the processing company may keep a small percentage of the gold output, as well as the sludge which still contains a lot of gold. An even better equipped company, which has the possibility of processing the sludge by chemical treatment, will make huge profits by just processing the waste of small-scale miners. Some listed companies like DRG Gold and New Dawn Mining have already successfully started this business in Zimbabwe. But there is room for more.

This is a small-scale gold mine in Zimbabwe, close to Kadoma. (Photo by: Hartmut Sieper)

This option is not out of range for middle class Americans, as individuals or groups. Lauri is aware of several upper middle class African-American professionals, who own gold mines across Africa. They were not big-name, multi-millionaires to start.

Seeing this as a "hidden" opportunity that God has given us, we have organized gold projects to be implemented on an adapted model of one successful African-American, who is gold mining, with the idea of being able to replicate them across the continent.

Besides small-scale gold mining, we will scan certain regions of these and other countries to identify additional areas with mineral resources and apply for prospecting licenses. In this respect, a sophisticated new reconnaissance technology for mineral resources, which was developed by a German believer, might play a decisive role. I connected with this person in 2010, after having received a personal prophecy in Zambia in 2007 which pinpointed to this man in a very special way. I'm quite positive that this project has the potential of becoming a vessel for the transfer of wealth, according to the Bible.

In order to make a difference from the old business model of exploiting Africa, the project owners will tithe 10% of the net profits and will invest a further 20% into other viable projects locally, especially in agriculture and drinking water supply. By wisely using the natural wealth, it will be possible to uplift people, communities, regions, and countries.

As these projects are for-profit enterprises, development aid is not needed. Projects of this kind require investors, not donors. Only viable, profitable projects can be and should be multiplied.

As believers, the triple bottom line – profit, people, and planet - should be mandatory for us. I am deeply convinced that we have the role of gatekeepers. We have to keep the enemy out of heavenly projects. As glittering gold over centuries triggered greed, and gold rushes have attracted many people with the wrong motives, the sharp edge is obvious. Before investing into mining and exploration, you should ask the Lord for the right motives.

Conclusion

Genesis 2 speaks of the four rivers pouring out from the river of the Garden of Eden, including the river Pishon. This river surrounds the land of Havilah. Pishon means "increase". Havilah means "gold". So, there are places on this earth which help us to increase and are associated with gold. One of these places is Africa.

Gold's benefits include being a rare mineral that cannot be substituted, a tradable asset, and not "fiat" money. There is a wealth of it in Africa.

We only have to imagine the gold rushes in the U.S. West in the 1800s to imagine the potential in Africa, which has more deposits than the U.S. There are assets lying fallow just for us.

The winners in the U.S. gold rushes were those who got in early and found the sources of gold, as well as those who found a niche in the gold industry ecosystem like shipping companies, shovel makers, and minters. In the case of Africa and our work, this will increase us but will also free communities in which Christian churches operate and serve.

As I mentioned before, your motives should be right before God, but your reasons may vary. You may choose to do it to increase your own wealth to support your Kingdom work or to help communities in Africa develop sustainable livelihoods. And while gold may not be what you are led to pursue as an opportunity, you must look around you for the opportunities that lie fallow with which God has blessed you.

5

African Consumer Markets:
An Emerging "Gold" Mine
Nissi Ekpott

Africa's population is estimated at over a billion people, about 17% of the world's population, and is said to be the "youngest" globally. According to United Nations (UN) statistics, 43% of the population is young. Uganda is an extreme example of a young and fertile population. The median age is 15, and the population growth rate amounts to 3.56 % per year (2010 estimate). 6.73 children are born per woman, which is the second highest rate in the world.

Africa's economy measured in GDP per capita is larger than that of India. Also, the income per capita in about 20 countries is higher than that of China. These twenty nations, including South Africa, Botswana, Mauritius, Tunisia, and Ghana, make up a population of between 200 and 300 million Africans, according to Vijay Mahajan, author of *Africa Rising*.

The fact is that African consumers offer more than most people realize, but why do most people not realize what the continent offers? One major reason is because a staggering 400 to 500 million Africans are said to live on less than $2 per day. Much focus in discussion and activism in the past was placed on Africa's poverty, and most media features on Africa focus on this segment of the population which is poor.

Most people got distracted by this and failed to recognize the other 500 million people driving the economy of the continent. The truth is that this richer group has the potential to lift the poorer group out of poverty. One way this will be achieved is by recognizing this potential and investing in it.

Potential investors, especially those who have little experience with Africa, may ask several questions which will be addressed in this chapter:

- How can this consumer base be proven?
- Can consumers be relied on to purchase goods and services?
- Where in Africa can these consumers be found?
- How best can they be reached?
- Is there potential in consumers in poverty?
- What is the future in African consumer markets?
- How should Christians tap into the consumer markets?

Can This Consumer Base be Proven?

Mahajan points out that advertising agencies, economists, and researchers on the continent classify the market into five segments - A to E. Class A and B make up the upper and upper middle class, consisting of 5%-15% of the population, or 50-150 million people. This class consists of people who could be living anywhere in the world. They have access to resources, and are senior executives, foreign expatriates, small business owners, and entrepreneurs.

Class C consists of 35%-45% of the population, or 350-450 million people, mostly blue/white collar workers and self-employed, small-scale entrepreneurs. These people are as ambitious as anyone else in the world, as well as being optimistic, wanting the best for their kids, and believing in the future of the continent.

Combining these three classes, Africa presents a 400-500 million consumer market with cash flow that exceeds the United States and the European Union in size but not assets.

Senior fellow Vijaya Ramachandran, at the Center for Global Development (CGD), defines Africa's middle class as those living on more than $5 per day. Above $5 a day would not be enough income to be included in the middle class in the U.S., or other developed countries, but Ramachandran says it is sufficient to be part of Africa's "aspirational class". Ramachandran describes this middle class as having escaped the worst burdens of poverty, able to meet their basic needs in nutrition, health, and housing, not so insecure, and do not risk losing this on a daily basis, which is what it is like for those existing on less than $5 per day.[35]

Going by these estimates, the middle class contributes about $150-$225 billion annually into Africa's economy. This market size should automatically attract any investor in the near and long term.

Another drawing card is the youthfulness of the continent's population. Some researchers refer to them as the Cheetah generation. The Cheetah generation was probably first coined by George Ayittey in his book, *Africa Unchained*[36].

This generation is not bogged down by the baggage of the colonial past - they are ambitious, optimistic, and colorful. For them, the sky is the limit. They are fast gaining access to mobile phones and the Internet. With these new technologies, they are getting to be at par with the rest of the world. Many of them, though having little

---

[35] Meldrum, A. (May 19, 2010). Africa's Middle Class: Striving to Develop a Continent. *Global Post.* Accessed online at http://www.globalpost.com/dispatch/africa/100514/africa%E2%80%99s-middle-class-striving-develop-continent (January 28, 2011).

[36] Ayittey, G. (2006). *Africa Unchained: The Blueprint for Africa's Future.* New York, NY: Palgrave McMillan.

now, are actively working to be significant economic players and consumers of the near future.

No better example of the potential of African consumer markets, including the Cheetah generation, is the rapid growth of mobile phone users from 54 million in 2003 to close to 350 million in 2008.[37] The number of mobile phone users is fast approaching half a billion. This rapid growth has confounded skeptics who believed the uptake would be poor based on the idea that a consumer base did not exist.

The Second, or Informal, Economy

The second economy is also referred to as the parallel, underground, or informal economy. These are productive and unproductive activities that are not captured by official statistics. The second economy in Africa is large and vibrant.

Naturally, the true size of this economy is not known because it's a hidden economy, so estimates vary from 30% to as high as 80% of economic activity in different parts of the continent. Many key economic players have remained in this sector to escape the brunt of harsh economic policies, influenced mostly by economic decisions of the past (especially between the 70s and 90s where many of the national economic policies had the effect of crippling business).

The picture has shifted though. From 2000 until recently, some African countries have been on the forefront of economic reforms. Rwanda, for instance, was rated number one globally for improvements in economic reforms in 2010, according to the Doingbusiness.org website.

---

[37] Smith, D. (October 22, 2009). Africa Calling: Mobile Phone Usage Sees Record Rise After Huge Investment. *The Guardian*. Accessed online at http://www.guardian.co.uk/technology/2009/oct/22/africa-mobile-phones-usage-rise (January 11, 2011).

This increasing rate of reforms offers hope that many of the second economy players will be integrated into the proper economy, able to enjoy the benefits while contributing to the building of these economies. A lot of Africa's consumer market potential lies in being able to harness the wealth within this market.

In South Africa, the community savings scheme of stokvels is worth over 4.8 billion Rand (~$738 million) per year, according to the National Stockvel Association of South Africa (NASASA). Community, or informal, savings schemes exist all over Africa with a focus on preparing for major life events like birth, marriage, and death. As a business person, if you provide a product or service for this segment you have tapped into a market with ready cash as long as the product or service serves the goal of those saving.

One key ingredient for the success of the mobile telephone companies across the continent was the ability to bridge the economic divide between "first" and "second" economies. For example, telephone services were typically offered on a contract basis to customers who were to make payments on a monthly basis. Mobile telephone operators introduced prepaid mobile phone service, which opened the door for the operators into the second economy.

In South Africa, only about 20% of the population could access contract services. The reason being that to obtain a contract, a user needed to meet certain basic documentation requirements. Most users were sidelined. For instance, many of them resided in underdeveloped slums without proper home addresses. The result was that typical users were those from the first, or visible, economy.

With prepaid service programs, anyone with money can now use mobile phones. The result has been rapid growth in mobile phone penetration in South Africa, which is estimated to be over 100%. Many other African countries also have rapidly growing penetration rates, Gabon and Seychelles have also reached 100% penetration. In

Uganda, the penetration rate rose from 0.5% in 1995 to 23% in 2008.[38] Only five countries in Africa, Burundi, Djibouti, Eritrea, Ethiopia, and Somalia, have a penetration rate less than 10%.

Robert Neuwirth, in *Shadow Cities*[39], estimates the informal economy in the city of Lagos, Nigeria to contribute about $125 billion to the economy of the nation, and 80% of jobs. This is certainly potential that cannot be brushed aside.

Can Consumers be Relied Upon to Buy?

Mahajan found that African consumers were looking for goods and services just like any other consumer globally. When he did further study, he was surprised to discover that a large number of western and global business corporations were already present and well entrenched in Africa, supplying goods and services.

What was a surprise to Professor Mahajan is a fact every resident on the continent has always known. Africans joke about the reach of Coca-Cola, saying that the drink can be found in every province, region, and rural community in Africa. This has been a fact for a long time and applies to several other products and brands.

The key challenge for service providers is how to innovate their products in such a way as to make them affordable for communities of people, whose disposable income is not as large as traditional Western markets.

For instance, Coca-Cola sells its drinks in re-usable bottles. The drinks are sold as "liquid content only". This means that for a buyer to buy a bottle of Coke, he exchanges his empty bottle for a new, unopened bottle. He is buying only the liquid content. This way he

---

[38] Ibid.
[39] Neuwirth, R. (2004). *Shadow Cities: A Billion Squatters, A New Urban World.* London: Routledge.

does not have to pay for the cost of the bottle. In addition, bottles are small and easier to afford.

Vodacom Congo CEO Alieu Conteh, speaking in the *Africa Open for Business* documentary, says the company did research to discover that the average micro retailer had daily stock of goods valued at $5-$10. This led the company to consider reducing the value of prepaid airtime cards to $2. Immediately after this step, the number of users tripled. The number of users grew from 35,000 in the first week of operation to over 850,000 in its first two years.

Another example is the consumption of Chinese-made consumer items. Consumption has grown exponentially in the past few years, simply because the Chinese have understood this pricing concept. Having come from a country whose poverty rates and economic history share similarities with Africa, Chinese business people have the innate understanding of how to reach and leverage the mass market.

China-Africa trade has grown from $10 billion in the year 2000 to over $100 billion in 2010. A large chunk of this growth has to do with the importation of cheap Chinese products.

In a number of African countries, the Chinese trade model is already moving beyond exporting goods to Africa. Chinese companies are building factories right at the doorsteps of African consumers. They are employing strategies that keep their products affordable, and they are getting the returns.

In Nigeria[40] for instance, UAC, one of the biggest consumer product manufacturers, has spent over $40 million building a water bottling plant. The plant was so large it had to be built 300 kilometers (~186 miles) from Lagos, the bustling commercial capital. However, the distance and initial cost will make its water more costly than that of the Chinese company situated right in the heart of Lagos and which started operations with $300,000. The Chinese company is obviously thriving.

Businesses focused on providing consumer goods and services that meet basic needs at the right prices will have potential for good returns. The consumers are ready to buy because, in many cases, they have no alternatives. There is high demand, but constrained supply.

Mike Koester, a U.S. farmer on a recent visit to Southern Nigeria, its richest oil region, was surprised to discover that there was no source of fresh milk in a region with a population of over 20-30 million people. Such untapped industries abound across Africa.

---

[40] To get a better understanding of Nigerian consumer markets, view the on-demand webinar, "Understanding the Business Opportunities in the Nigerian Consumer Markets," at http://www.afribiz.info/content/understanding-the-business-opportunities-in-the-nigerian-consumer-markets. For other African consumer market information, check out http://www.afribiz.info/insightareas/consumer-markets.

Where Can Consumers Be Found in Africa?

This is a busy intersection in Uyo, Akwa Ibom State in Nigeria. (Photo by: Hartmut Sieper)

A fact, which may surprise the average Western business person, is the African consumer market consists of consumers located in EVERY country of the continent. The typical reports of bad news overshadow and hide the fact that products and services are in demand everywhere, albeit distributed from major hubs.

For instance, Johannesburg, South Africa is fast becoming the "Dubai of Africa," a shopping destination for consumers from the Southern African region of over 200 million people.

These people previously needed to travel to Dubai to shop for some of their needs, including clothing and accessories, cell phones, electronic products, computers, etc. Most of these consumers are themselves resellers within their home communities.

This is a view of Johannesburg Central Business District from Nelson Mandela Bridge. (Photo by: Nissi Ekpott)

Producers and suppliers of these products took up retail space within the Johannesburg Central Business District (CBD), and hence cut out the need for a trip to Dubai. This enabled traders from South Africa and from every other Southern African country easy access to these products.

A trader from, say Malawi, only has to do a road trip to Johannesburg to buy his stock. His travel expenses are significantly lower than having to travel all the way to Dubai. It is estimated that over 400,000 people daily travel the streets of the Johannesburg CBD looking for trade deals, and the numbers are growing. The traders' activities energize demand for other services, such as transport, freight, hotels, food, etc.

Lagos, Nigeria is another hub in West Africa. Traders from the region troop to various major markets in Lagos for their supplies, cutting out the need for them to travel to China and other sources of these goods. And as Africa becomes more urbanized, these business hubs will continue to spur economic activity.

Business strategists realize that though there are pockets of consumers all across the continent, the small scale is sometimes unattractive. To overcome these challenges, companies are beginning to look at approaching a combination of markets at one time. There are already regional economic communities, e.g., COMESA, SADC, Maghreb Union, and ECOWAS, which offer a basis for developing strategies for trade.

The Market Potential of the Poor

Approximately 500 million Africans are said to live on less than $2 a day. These are said to be poor people. They are those whom the world has learned to pity. Many of them live in slums and in rural areas.

However, there is a fact the casual observer fails to grasp. This is the fact that a dollar in Africa goes further than a dollar in the U.S. This may render the $2/day measure insignificant when considering business opportunities.

Services in Africa are very cheap compared to the West. A haircut in Cameroon costs 50 cents or less. This would be unheard of anywhere in the U.S. Many other services are equally cheap. These Africans, who live below $2 a day, either patronize these cheap services or, in many cases, device innovative ways to acquire goods and services without exchanging cash. For example, two people might barter to cut each other's hair, or one person exchanges a fish with a person for grain.

Poor consumers innovate to make the most of what they have. They do as Moses was instructed – use what they have available. Rural dwellers supplement their food needs from small gardens and farms. The market is big on do-it-yourself and home-made solutions, e.g., people fix their broken appliances and build their shanty homes with used sheets or in rural areas with mud.

Community-based solutions can include whole communities collaborating to build homes for each person who needs one. In the rural areas, these are mud homes which require very little maintenance. The amount of money spent on these homes is zero.

Another example is stokvels and thrift societies. These are community banks and lending institutions where participants make contributions at agreed periods and the total contributions are given to each participant in turn until everyone has got a turn. As mentioned before, a study indicated that this informal sector was worth over 4 billion Rand annually in South Africa.

The poor consumer can be characterized with having zero bills. Many do not have monthly bills and they use only what they can afford. If they own phones, they use prepaid airtime. They often will get free education sponsored by the state or development and aid agencies. They live simple lives with minimal needs.

With this type of lifestyle, $2/day becomes a reasonable amount of money and eventually goes into the needs that cannot be provided locally, such as clothes, beverages, improved housing, further education, food, and other basic needs.

In fact, you can find many "luxury" items in African villages where people earning less than $2/day could not normally afford. These luxury items include millions of radios, TVs, lots of Coca-Cola, etc.

If 100 million poor people are able to live on one dollar a day, $100 million is circulating through the economies of the poor daily. In a year, this comes to over $30 billion, quite a significant amount of money.

The challenge facing the investor is how to identify the needs of the poor, and supply these needs at affordable prices. In addition, if the need meeting strategies are able to create jobs for the poor, then the virtuous cycle is in place with the potential to lift whole economies out of poverty and help businesses create and empower their own consumers to increase their buying power.[41]

It is interesting to note that even war-torn communities continue to play economically. There is something about humanity and economics, people find ways to be active as long as they have life. A community with no economic activity would only be one that has dead people – the graveyard.

How Do You Find Basic Statistics on Consumer Markets?

It is necessary to note that statistical inefficiencies exist in many parts of Africa. Unlike in developed markets where statistics can be relied on, many African nations have recently emerged from one form of conflict or another, and many of them though in the process of rebuilding social, economic, and administrative systems are still way short of best practices.

Though there's still some way to go, international institutions like the World Bank, International Monetary Fund, African Development Bank, and United Nations agencies have committed vast resources to collect data, as well as strengthen African institutions to improve on data collection. It is this data that enable most economists to safely estimate the size of the market within tolerable error margins.

Any investor planning to get involved in Africa needs to grasp one fact that may sometimes not be obvious – speed. Whenever things

---

[41] For further information on developing strategies to create your own consumers in Africa, read the "Creating Your Own Consumers" chapter in *Redefining Business in the New Africa* (http://www.redefining-business-in-the-new-africa.com). You can also listen to interview conduct by Lauri Elliott with Johnny Goldberg, an expert on empowerment in South Africa, at http://www.blogtalkradio.com/afribiz/2010/06/16/creating-your-consumers-in-africa-matching-people-and-profits.

begin to change in an African nation, they change rapidly. With the aid of technology, African nations are simply leapfrogging the development cycle. Research and data collection have not been able to keep up.

One of the challenges Africa faces in attracting investment is that before the "golden decade" recognized as 2000-2010, where African economies have experienced greater growth than any other time in modern history, African nations had years of stagnation and negative growth. Investment in research was very minimal, the data usually outdated. In saying this, it's pertinent to note that there are a number of African nations, such as South Africa, whose statistics are of high reliability. From these nations, accurate estimates can be made of the size and characteristics of the consumer markets.

Economic decisions are not necessarily in tandem with current events at the grassroots level because data has not been available. As with any business opportunity and in this case in particular, you will want to do your own market research. But you have the best field personnel available to you – Christian church, parachurch, and missions organizations spread throughout Africa.

Future of the African Consumer in the Global Economy

Any keen observer will notice a disturbing, but real trend in the economic architecture of the world today - the average Western consumer has reached a peak, and is most likely to be on a consumption downtrend for a long time until a lot of economic anomalies are corrected.

A look at the world debt trend, in The Economist, indicates that the world's richest nations have taken up the greatest amount of debt.[42] Some economies today have a debt-to-GDP ratio of over 200%. The United States has an overall debt-to-GDP ratio of about 259%.

This indicates that the ability to consume is seriously threatened in the medium and long terms. An economic implosion is of a very high probability. If this happens, consumption patterns will change radically and the buying power of the average individual will be seriously diminished.

On the other hand, if affected countries decide to forestall this implosion by introducing corrective measures, the result will be serious changes in consumer behavior leading to further economic slowdowns. Many economists agree that this is inevitable. The question is when.

What does this mean? Investors and business people need to look at new markets. These new markets will serve to keep Western-owned businesses stable until their nations' economic situations correct. With this in mind, the world is looking at a potential "savior" from economic crises.

Developing economies of Africa, Asia, and South America offer opportunities. Mahajan puts forward an astounding observation - African economies, taken collectively, represent the world's tenth largest economy in terms of GDP! Of course, this needs to be taken in perspective as true economic unity is yet to happen across national borders. However, with the growth of trade blocs, it is only a matter of time until this economic integration happens.

---

[42] Buttonwood. (June 24, 2010). World Debt. *The Economist.* Accessed online at http://www.economist.com/blogs/buttonwood/2010/06/ indebtedness_after_financial_crisis (January 11, 2011).

This potentially large economy is sitting largely underdeveloped, requiring vast amounts of investment but possessing enormous potential for high returns. Africa has the capacity to absorb new investments, skills, technology, goods, and services for a long time.

It also has the potential to become the future breadbasket for the world. Its resources are still largely untapped in a world that is fast running low of resources.

As new industries spring up on the continent, a virtuous cycle is created - workers are employed, new consumers are added, who in turn need new products and services. In this information age, the continent will leapfrog the development cycle.

How Best to Tap the African Consumer Markets

Tapping into the hidden wealth offered by the African consumer markets requires a mindset shift. Large corporations have known this and have been in Africa for decades, right through the darkest of times. Today, opportunities are also opening up for small and medium-size enterprises. Christians should consider the following when tapping these markets.

See beyond Images of Poverty, Conflict, and Corruption

The business decision makers need to see Africa beyond the caricature images of poverty seen on TV. They need to recognize the fundamental changes on the continent, which still has many problems. And, they need to be comfortable with Africa already being on an upward growth trajectory.

Recognize Potential of Growing Youth Population

An investor needs to recognize the potential of a growing youthful population, which offers long-term potential. Then, develop strategies to access this market.

Design Innovative Solutions to Harness Potential of Market

An investor has to design innovative solutions to harness this potential market. The African terrain is very challenging - tough, underdeveloped in many cases, and with multiple issues that could hinder business. Without an above average emphasis on innovation, any African foray is doomed to fail.

South African companies have succeeded in this space; they are involved in over 2,000 projects across the continent. South Africa is among the biggest investors on the continent, if not the biggest.

Alan Knot Craig, former Vodacom CEO, tells the story of deploying mobile phone base stations across rural areas, jungles, war-torn areas, etc. They found ways of being able to overcome the variety of problems in each of the nations.

Innovation should not be limited to product and service offerings only, but has to extend to pricing. It is important to look at ways of making it cheaper.

Craig's story reflects one that is very common across the face of the continent. The level of innovation available at all levels in Africa is simply astounding. You cannot grasp it until you see it.

Know the Market and Develop Appropriate Strategies

Look beyond some of the "impossible" challenges and pictures painted by media. Get on the ground and find out things for yourself. Do your own research. Look for value in the rough diamond. Learn from businesses, which are in Africa already.

You need to be able to reach African consumers at their level, offering them products they can identify with, and gradually guiding them up to what you see as global best standards.

Carry out thorough research of your target market, combining your personal research with information from other sources. Make wise business decisions, limiting risk and boosting impact.

The markets are usually fragmented and underdeveloped, if not undeveloped. Develop strategy to organize the market. Start from major hubs and work outwards.

Leverage the African Diaspora

Recognize and tap into the hidden strength of the African diaspora. It can bring resources and knowledge to create successful strategies for business in Africa.

Leverage African Culture

Investors should understand and leverage on Africa's culture, taking advantage of social, faith-based, professional, and other networks, which are an inherent part of African culture. These cultural networks are one of the most powerful means to furthering any initiative and spreading any message.

Focus on the Long Term

Invest for the long term. Systems in Africa are not efficient in general, but improving. Things take longer than they normally should. This should not be a deterrent. The market takes longer to develop, but a long-term outlook will put an investor in a good place.

The Christian Business Person and Africa

There is growing confidence among African Christians, who believe that the continent of Africa is poised to take up the mantle and move to the forefront of world missions. This belief is strengthened by the fast growth of African-led churches in various parts of the world, including in the U.S. The African Church is fast finding its feet and rising up to express itself in a powerful way, locally and internationally.

Most foreign Christian business people are still only engaging with Africa through charity via their various churches, or other ministries. They have a passion to help, but many have not fully grasped the fact that the best help one can give is to invest in Africa.

The global Christian community, in partnership with their African brethren, needs to step into the forefront of a new approach to Africa. Christianity has had the greatest influence on the continent, and the vast existing network of Christians within the society gives the Church a potential reach that is much wider than any other institution currently. With a population of over 400 million church-going people, Christian business leaders have unending possibilities at their disposal, waiting to be harnessed.

The way to go is move beyond the charity-and-aid-only approach into a business building approach. For example, AGOA was established over a decade ago to promote African exports to the U.S. It has helped mostly the exports of commodities.

One sector that has benefited from AGOA was the clothing industry in Lesotho. This industry employs over 50,000 people. The multiplier effect could result in food on the table and clothes on the backs of over 500,000 people. Very few aid agencies, if any, are able to achieve such results on a sustainable basis.

NeuAfrika analysts say that a 3%-5% increase in Africa's participation in global trade has the potential to reduce poverty by half. The Church, led by its business people, needs to re-examine its African strategy, and become smart about it. Channeling 25%-50% of support into projects could achieve tremendous gains while giving Christian business persons a solid business footing on the continent.

Business people generally tend to go where there's an opportunity, and so if charity money is channeled into business, they will follow. Better still, if the Church does the channeling, those who follow will be people who do not only do business, but do it in a way that transforms society morally.

Investing in Africa today is a window of opportunity for the Christian business person to get a stake in what promises to be one of the biggest assets of our day.

Conclusion

People are actually the greatest treasure any nation can have. We were made in God's image and Jesus died to save us. Yet, we often underestimate the potential to bless and be blessed through people.

This chapter illustrated how people are one of the "hidden" treasures in Africa, which God has stored up for this day. However, its population size has been considered a burden in the past. With the shift in global economies, this burden is now a visible blessing.

From the poorest to the richest person in Africa, the path in Africa is peppered with opportunities, but mindsets caught in the paradigms of the past will not be able to tap these opportunities well. Let the Lord transform your view of Africa's people as poor to potential, not only for their sake but for yours.

6

Transforming the Christian Faith Network for Business

Lauri Elliott

There is an under tapped channel to catalyze trade and economic development in Africa. It has existed for hundreds of years. Today, it readily and effectively responds to disaster after disaster around the world. It is a part of the civil society sphere, which is considered vital to a functioning society. This channel is the Christian faith network. In Africa, there are close to 500 million Christians and 400 million Muslims. These numbers account for 90% of the entire population.

The Christian faith is predominant in Sub-Saharan Africa. So, if you want to reach out to Africans for any reason, it's logical to tap the Christian faith network.

Some may have a hard time with this because in the West there is a vocal credo of the "separation of church and state"; whether it is truly legislated or really works is another issue. For example, it is known that when disaster strikes in the United States the National Voluntary Active Disaster (Vo-ad) network, comprised mostly of faith-related institutions, is a fast and effective responder. In fact, the Federal Emergency Management Agency (FEMA) in the United States signed a memorandum of understanding with Vo-ad to reach out to communities in disaster. In Haiti, there were already many faith organizations like Operation Blessing there and able to tap into their global networks to ramp up response.

And, if the truth be told, government and international aid organizations partner with local faith organizations to reach local populations in the developing world. Why? First, they understand and have become in varying degrees part of the local culture and people. Second, faith culture in developing nations is one of the most powerful social institutions.

Third, the Christian faith network has a way of reaching people even in very remote regions. Some Christian pastors and bishops establish churches in rural and remote regions. To reach these communities, they may have to walk or ride a motorcycle, but they do reach them.

So, if the Christian faith network can help address natural disasters, why can't they be tapped to address an even larger, continual disaster – poverty in Africa? To the audience that finds it hard to mix business and faith, poverty or untapped wealth in Africa is a continual disaster that needs to be addressed. From an economic standpoint, until Africa is able to tap its wealth more broadly there will continue to be an overreliance on aid.

In actuality, faith-based organizations already support economic development. Professor Nwabufo Uzodike, Head of the School of Politics at the University of KwaZulu-Natal, reports that the Catholic Church has stepped in to assist communities with economic development projects in the DRC because of insufficient government institutions. Also, large international aid organizations like World Vision embed economic development components in their community development projects.

Other faith-based organizations like Business Partners International and the Center for Entrepreneurship at Regent University's School of Business help develop small and medium enterprises in developing countries. In these instances, however, the goal is to serve the people by helping them get out of poverty.

What is not activated is positioning the Christian faith network as a market and economy. If we look at the aid sector, Western businesses already tap large aid, faith or non-faith, organizations as clients. So, in some realms this is already working, but at the same time the "aid" engine is perverted in some ways making some wealthy and keeping others in poverty. A friend of mine worked for a large U.S.-based aid organization in Sudan among refugees. She suggested that they help the refugees develop enterprises. She was told matter-of-factly they would not do so because it would put the organization out of business.

In a good example, CARE decided to no longer participate in some aspects of the World Food Programme (WFP) because they were not able to leverage their assets to catalyze economic opportunities as much for the communities they served. Through WFP, CARE might be paying more to foreign firms for what local businesses could supply more affordably while creating more opportunity for locals.

Fortunately, the traditional development formula may be changing in small ways, at least in the U.S. since one of the pillars of its development assistance is to catalyze sustainable economic growth. The Kauffman Foundation has even proposed using military resources to catalyze local economic development in post-conflict zones. Kauffman calls this "expeditionary" economics.

But beyond the argument for helping people get out of poverty is the importance of pulling people out of poverty for the global economy so everyone wins. Dambisa Moyo, author of *Dead Aid*, popularized the stance of "trade instead of aid" for Africa. While aid is helpful for development, it is not a sustainable solution.

And until this balances out, developed countries will likely continue to pour out aid to assist. These are the same countries who are reeling under debt like the U.S. and U.K. At some point, if there isn't a shift in this system, like the world financial systems, it will reel out of control and break, leaving more destruction in its path.

Trade, markets, and business, on the other hand, are the engines of thriving economies. Africa's poverty is systemic, so a systematic solution is needed not just pockets of solutions.

First, we need to identify and leverage existing systems that have enough momentum to catalyze economic opportunity. Second, we need to find ways to catalyze trade within these networks in Africa to create wealth instead of poverty, reducing reliance on aid.

Faith and business have co-existed for hundreds of years in Africa. The Islamic faith spread through Arab traders in Africa. While Christianity started in North Africa and Ethiopia many centuries before Islam, it did not spread into Sub-Saharan Africa in a major way until Europeans came to the continent. It is now time for the Christian Church to activate its position on the continent for the Kingdom wealth transfer promised by God, which will help not just our own but the world.

The Christian faith network is organized in local, regional, and global spaces, which can perhaps be considered markets not just faith communities or organizations. For example, local churches are normally under the leadership of a geographic administration, which in turn is connected to state, national, and international church administrations. There are also often direct connections between churches in developed nations to those in developing nations, focusing on specific projects like building schools, houses, and hospitals.

It also should be noted that, in the United States, faith is a specific market segment. There is a very strong Christian marketplace, including music, messages, books, etc. CBA, a Christian retail sector association, estimated that in 2006 Christian sales through its members exceeded $4.6 billion. This doesn't include sales in mainstream bookstores and discounters like Barnes and Noble and Wal-Mart. So, faith and the marketplace do mix. Why can't the social networks in the Christian faith network be leveraged for other economic pursuits on a more systematic and global scale, connecting one community at a time?

The Christian faith network can also bring an ethical framework, trust, and emphasis on people into the alternative market constructed around them. And, if anything, the importance of these factors in the wake of the global economic crisis should be self-evident.

So how would something like this work? One of the best markets to consider is agriculture because of Africa's ability to be a major agricultural consumer and producer. Africa has a growing population, increasing the demand for agricultural products.

In fact, agricultural production in Africa has the potential to serve world markets as well. The importance of agriculture to the world was felt with the food shortages and price spikes in the last several years. This has ignited greater interest in the agricultural sector, particularly in Africa which has a lot of virgin, arable land. The purchase of African land for agricultural development by foreign investors and governments is a normal occurrence now.

Unfortunately, the agricultural sector in Africa faces challenges, including low crop yields, distribution, and access to world markets, giving a very different picture. However, some improvements in the value chain have made a significance difference as was illustrated by the example of Malawi in Chapter 3: *Glaring Opportunities.*

If the U.S. Christian church turns its attention to this opportunity, there are consumers, businesses, and investors within this faith community that could tie into the African agricultural sector. Christian businessmen, specializing in agriculture and related sectors, could develop and/or invest in African agricultural projects for profit. U.S. Christians can take advantage of AGOA (to export products from Africa to U.S.) and other U.S. programs.

The Christian Church can also tie these business opportunities to communities they serve or provide aid to in Africa, helping develop sustainable livelihoods. This includes marketing, distributing, and selling the products among their networks. As an example, the Christian Reformed World Relief Committee advocates purchasing Fair Trade products.

Again, it's not that pieces of this puzzle are not already working in varying degrees, but it's not configured as a market or economy to leverage and maximize existing assets within it to benefit the broadest number of members in the Christian faith network whether in Africa or elsewhere. If it does represent a market or economy, it is fragmented.

And finally, while there are significant challenges and obstacles to taking this approach, the Christian faith network has many leverage points working in its favor, including existing infrastructure to distribute information and resources, funding for seeding agricultural projects which will bring a return on investment, and most of all, ecosystems of people who have the knowledge and expertise to make it happen.

The critical challenge at this time is for the Christian faith network and its members to transform their thinking and move out into the marketplace and see themselves as economies and markets with potential.

A Business Example for Leveraging the Christian Network

We see the vast potential of consumers in the over 1 billion people that live on the continent whether rich, middle income, or poor. Reaching the ends of this population is traditionally difficult and most in business avoid it. However, as mentioned before, the Christian Church has the most extensive network to reach the majority of communities in Sub-Saharan Africa.

The largest segment of this population – the poor – face challenges that make them seem unlikely consumers. The basic needs of healthy food and clean water are often seemingly insurmountable for them. Businesses in this African context need to develop new models for successful business that will be profitable for all key stakeholders, address the additional burdens of the African continent, and deliver products and services at high levels and within the context of the African continent.

One idea is to establish a continental virtual and physical network, connected by people, to deliver basic 'quality of' and 'critical' life products and services, such as clean water. The long-term business opportunity is to have a continental distribution network for products and services that are dispersed in every corner of the continent through local distributors and entrepreneurs. Thousands of other products and services can be delivered on top of this backbone now and even when infrastructure is no longer a major challenge.

In the current context, clean water is one of the major and critical issues for people living on the continent. Massive effort has been spent on addressing the issue yet little significant, systematic, sustainable solutions have remained for various reasons. Most of the channels and applications that deliver clean water are governmental/NGO/NPO/religious organizations based on a donation model. While good, it still has been woefully inadequate in the larger scheme of things. There seems to be little private sector activity directly to the consumers, perhaps because others see no profitable business model.

In our case, we see differently. Much work and research has evolved over the last two decades on delivering products and services to the poor as consumers instead of victims, which shows that tapping into this market is extremely profitable. The prime example in Africa is the mobile phone market.

In the instance of cleaning water, the best product is one in which individuals, families, and communities can afford, easily access, and easily use. In fact, there are several ministries like Hydromissions (www.hydromissions.com) and Aqua Clara (www.aquaclara.org), which provide products that can be used to access and/or clean water.

One possible business venture is starting a water cleaning and provisioning firm in the DRC with specific business line applications also in South Africa. We have recent direct data from both national and provincial governments in the DRC which says that at most 12% of the population of over 70 million people have clean drinking water. In every part of the country, access to clean drinking water is among the top three objectives for the next four to five years. There are plans in place but no immediate solution to the problem. This business venture brings the immediate solution.

Even if we only serve 5%-10% of the over 70 million people, the profit potential is huge in both tangible and intangible assets. Intangibly, we create a positive corporate image which means organizations and people will look to us for other solutions and products.

Also, we improve the quality of life for our consumers by eliminating probably the largest source of health problems. Unofficially, a chemist from the DRC, and working in a U.N. science office, said that if this worked we would solve 80% of the health issues among people in the DRC and 50% of the problems in children.

Even though infrastructure makes it difficult for us to penetrate the market geographically, the extreme need for the product to help people in the country can help bring strategic partners to get it done. And, the Christian Church is the only network that can reach almost any location in the DRC.

While this example may seem overpowering, remember that God gives us big visions and ideas, but has us start with what He has given us (e.g., Moses and his staff), which God uses supernaturally to produce incredible results. The next section looks at how you begin the process while the next chapter – Leveraging Trust Networks – shares how you build a business ecosystem, a few relationships at a time, to shape business strategy.

Framework for Leveraging Faith Networks for Business

The first phase is to focus on the "sacred". Ask for God's revelation in prayer and fasting. Perhaps you have already been doing so about your next move in business and you were waiting for something to touch your spirit? Always be led by the Holy Spirit and work in the flow of God, so that you reside in His covering, blessing, and grace. Look for a Word from the Lord that will guide your approach and decisions.

The second phase is to focus on strategy. And within the strategy framework, focus on the strengths, gifts, and people God has given you. Essentially, you need to leverage all your assets as God would have you do so. What do I mean by this?

The Leverage Point Strategy™ is a specific methodology, which I developed, based on the concept of leverage. Leverage is the ratio of change in input to the change in output. Greater leverage is gained when a small force multiplies output. The goal is to see a small force produce as much change in output as possible.

Leverage points are those forces, or points, that create the rate of change in output. The power of leverage points is on a continuum from low to high. The best scenario is to locate high leverage points, because, in these cases, the smallest amounts of force effect the greatest change or results.

A very clear picture of a leverage point is the rudder of a ship. It is a small part of the ship in comparison with the size of the ship, but it creates a small force that is able to turn the ship in a new direction. In practical terms, maximizing leverage points makes use of small, but significant, forces.

Leverage points are related to tipping points. A tipping point is a point at which an object is displaced from one place to a new and different state. Leverage points are used to create the tipping point.

Malcolm Gladwell wrote the book *The Tipping Point: How Little Things Make a Big Difference*[43]. He identified three key factors, or types of leverage points, for creating tipping points: the Law of the Few, the Stickiness Factor, and the Power of Context.

The Law of the Few is when a few key types of people champion and catalyze an idea or concept to critical mass. The types of people are Connectors, Mavens, and Salesmen. When all three types of actors advocate an idea, the concept is more likely to reach a tipping point. Connectors, Mavens, and Salesmen are examples of leverage points. Each is a small force that can wield significant results.

The Stickiness Factor is something that sticks in the minds of individuals and influences their behavior in the future. And the

---

[43] Gladwell, M. (2002). *The Tipping Point: How Little Things Make a Big Difference*. New York, NY: Back Bay Books (Hatchette Book Group).

Power of Context is when the right environment, or time, aligns with your business opportunity to create momentum.

Each of the leverage points highlighted by Gladwell can induce a tipping point, but it is more likely that the combination of these leverage points will actually force a tipping point.

Another category of leverage points is types of capital. In essence, these are the strengths you bring to the business opportunity overall. According to Dr. Bruce Cook of Kingdom Venture Capital, there are 13 types of capital:

- **Economic** includes currency, liquid assets, and finance.
- **Social** includes community-focused or social good activities, such as relief work, charity, and scientific research.
- **Spiritual** refers to strength drawn from faith.
- **Knowledge** is what you and your team know, both the intellectual and mental processes.
- **Political** refers to formal political affiliations and influence.
- **Environmental** refers to assets in the global "green" movement, like carbon credits.
- **Creative** includes your creativity, artistic expression, and intellectual property.
- **Positional** refers to the roles, titles, and authority you hold both formally and informally.
- **Institutional** includes formal reputation, influence, status, alliances, and partners.
- **Physical** refers to your body's capacity, including energy and fitness.
- **Generational** refers to legacy, heritage, family lineage, and wealth that are passed down in families.

- **Closeness** refers to the ability to draw close and also to be vulnerable, or open, in relationships.
- **Relational** refers to the span and depth of your relationships both vertically and horizontally.

You may wonder how some types of capital (e.g., social) can serve as leverage points for business, but any form of capital can exert influence over business opportunities. For example, a young African-American attorney, Carlton Owens, moved to Ghana and established a gold mine. His gold mine sits on land on which a local indigenous tribe lives. In addition to getting a mining concession from the government, he had to form an agreement with the local chief on how the operation would benefit the community beyond jobs. Carlton agreed to build a school, among other things. In emerging markets, business is not separated from the complex system of society.

In actuality, many things are leverage points, including situations and circumstances. However, the leverage point might be in your favor or in someone else's, and the leverage point may have low or high impact. Your goal is to find a series of leverage points in your favor with high-impact potential.

The process of applying the Leverage Point Strategy™ works in conjunction with completing an environmental analysis, as well as a SWOT analysis, of your opportunities. Following these analyses, apply the Leverage Point Strategy™ by asking yourself the following questions:

- What are the key leverage points that will make an opportunity work?
- Which of the key leverage points have high, medium, or low impact?
- Which combinations of key leverage points will have the most impact?

- How will the key leverage points help to override the weaknesses and threats in an opportunity?
- In general, how will I incorporate the high-leverage points and high-leverage-point combinations into the business model?
- How will I know if the leverage points are working?

Once you have applied the Leverage Point Strategy™ to your analysis of opportunities, incorporate the leverage points into your business model appropriately. The business model gives a complete picture of how to implement the business successfully. It answers the question, "How do you logically create value?" Johan Wallin, in the book *Business Orchestration: Strategic Leadership in the Era of Digital Convergence*[44], says a business model:

> ...*defines the value-creation priorities of an actor (business) in respect to the utilization of both internal and external resources. It defines how the actor (business) relates with stakeholders, such as actual and potential customers, employees, unions, suppliers, competitors and other internal groups. It takes account of situations where the actor's (business') activities may (a) affect the business environment and its own business in ways that create conflicting interests, or impose risks on the actor (business) or (b) develop new, previously unpredicted ways of creating value.*

---

[44] Wallin, J. (2006). *Business Orchestration: Strategic Leadership in the Era of Digital Convergence*. New York, NY: Wiley.

In the book *Business Model Generation: A Handbook for Visionaries, Game Changers, and Challengers*[45], Alexander Osterwalder and Yves Pigneur pose key questions to consider when developing a solid business model. The following is an adaptation focused on leverage points: "What key leverage points will you use to…"

- Activate your customer segments?
- Maximize your revenue streams?
- Improve offerings for your customer segments?
- Better relate to your customers over time?
- Maximize resource allocation to run the business?
- Improve efficiency and effectiveness of key activities in running the business?
- Better utilize and leverage the "people" assets used to run the business?
- Increase and improve outputs of key activities?
- Maximize partnerships, alliances, and collaboration?
- Maximize network and distribution channels to reach customers?
- Manage and reduce costs of running the business?

Leverage points are simply tangible and intangible assets, resources, situations, etc. that can be used to gain and sustain momentum in the business environment. As you analyze a business opportunity or problem, identify leverage points. And use leverage points to help you assess opportunities, as well as incorporate the best leverage points and combinations into the business model and operations.

---

[45] Osterwalder, A., & Pigneur, Y. (2010). *Business Model Generation: A Handbook for Visionaries, Game Changers, and Challengers*. New York, NY: Wiley.

And the third phase is to focus on the solution to implement. In many cases, the best place to start with unknown territory is with those who have navigated it well before, and/or develop proof-of-concept business ventures to get your foot in the door.[46]

Conclusion

Reaching markets broadly across Africa can be a daunting task, yet God has seen to it that two mechanisms can do it rapidly and effectively, ICT and the Christian Church. The Church can reach places that even the Internet cannot quite penetrate in Africa. God has positioned the Church well for the wealth transfer that will happen through Africa for God's purposes, Africa's benefit, and to the rest of the world.

Joel Osteen recently taught on God placing things near you, the ordinary, to help you do the extraordinary. We, as Christians, take for granted the powerful network that God has placed in our hands and don't consider how this one network can change everything in the Kingdom and in Africa. Each of us needs to ask God, "Help me to see what you have put at my disposal?" says Joel Osteen.

In my own experience, I have had to train myself to see the "adjacent" opportunities as they are called by Ron Schultz, author of *Open Boundaries*[47] and *Adjacent Opportunities*[48]. Often people ask me how I made it so far with so few resources at the time. I learned the strategies of use what you have in your hand, tap into networks, and create new business scenarios from available assets.

---

[46] For further details on how to shape strategies and solutions for business in Africa and emerging markets, visit http://www.goingglobalonadime.com.

[47] Sherman, H., & Schultz, R. (1999). *Open Boundaries: Creating Business Innovation through Complexity*. New York, NY: Basic Books.

[48] Schultz, R. (2010). *Adjacent Opportunities: Sparking Emergent Social Action*. Litchfield, AZ: Emergent Publications.

Simply put, I create new ventures from configurations that may or may not exist. We all can do this. We are made in the image of God. God is the Creator, therefore we are creators. Go out and create something!

7

Leveraging Trust Networks

Lauri Elliott

On any day, you will find people exchanging things of value. A typical picture is a person buying a product from a vendor with cash or credit. However, value can be exchanged in a variety of ways including exchanges of information, services, resources, and products. Exchanges happen between individuals, businesses, organizations, and governments at inconceivable rates of speed, particularly with the advent of electronic payment systems and the Internet.

While the idea of exchanging value may be a simple concept, it is played out in a complex environment. For example, the value chain to deliver cars to customers involves an entire ecosystem of agents, people, and organizations. There are the designers and engineers that draw the blueprint for the car. There are firms that transform raw materials into parts. There are other firms that take parts and transform them into components. Then, there are firms that assemble the vehicles. And consider the transport, distribution, and sales systems which support the entire value chain.

One common denominator in all forms of value exchange is trust. Both sides of the exchange trust they are getting the value expected from the exchange, trusting each other to provide the value expected or agreed upon. According to Merriam-Webster, trust is the "assured reliance on the character, ability, strength, or truth of someone or something."

Kenneth Arrow, an international economist, said as economic and social interactions become more complex, trust becomes the lubricant to keep things moving.[49] Oil lubricates engine parts to reduce friction between moving parts while improving efficiency and reducing wear, trust does similarly for business transactions, markets, and economic systems.

Anthony Giddens said that as societal and organizational processes modernize trust also becomes more important.[50] Georg Simmel suggests that individual and collective wealth would not exist today without trust.[51]

If trust is so important to economic interaction, can it be used to leverage global business opportunities? And if so, how can it be used?

In fact, trust is already leveraged to take advantage of global business opportunities. The example that affects all of us is "fiat" money. Fiat money, which is typically thought of as paper but also includes coins, is currency which a government decrees is legal tender. Fiat money has no intrinsic value but we trust the government issuing the currency is backed by something of value.

We can look to the recent example of Zimbabwe to see when fiat money is not backed by something of value and a government is not trusted to deliver something of value against it. Zimbabwe experienced hyperinflation in the latter half of the first decade of the 21st century. The Zimbabwean government continued to print more bank notes without any evidence they were backed by something of value. At one point in 2009, the government planned to issue different denominations of (e.g. 10, 50) trillion Zimbabwean dollar notes, which would have been valued well below $100.

---

[49] Arrow, K. (1974). *Limits of Organization.* New York: W.W. Norton & Company.
[50] Giddens, A. (1990). *The Consequences of Modernity.* Stanford, CA: Stanford University Press.
[51] Simmel, G. (1978). *The Philosophy of Money.* London: Routledge & Kegan Paul.

More and more businesses and people began to use foreign currency, refusing to accept Zimbabwe's local currency. People even exchanged mobile phone minute scratch cards as a form of currency. They no longer trusted in Zimbabwe's legal tender. In the end, Zimbabwe stopped circulation of its local currency and the U.S. Dollar and South African Rand became the country's legal tender, along (theoretically) with the Euro and the British Pound.

This example illustrates trust at work in major systems, but there are many practical examples in everyday business. A manager who delegates tasks to sub-ordinates, but then micromanages them, does not trust them. Micromanagement leads to de-motivation and bad team dynamics, which ultimately will cost.

There are other ways that trust can be leveraged to do global business. Research has shown that trust improves negotiations, increases flow of information, increases ability to learn, increases flexibility in management, increases speed of business transactions, and reduces costs, such as costs of transaction, governing relationships, agency, and opportunity.[52]

Trust is actually a strategic resource, according to Jay Barney and Mark Hansen, and can lead to competitive advantage when strong trust exists.[53] But more than a resource that can be used up and depleted, it is a strategic asset that if developed and managed correctly will only grow.

---

[52] Bachmann, R., & Zaheer, A. (eds.) (2006). *Handbook of Trust Research*. Cheltenham, UK: Edward Elgar Publishing.
[53] Barney, J.B., & Hansen, M.H. (1994). Trustworthiness as a Source of Competitive Advantage. *Strategic Management Journal, 15*, 175-190.

Imagine being a firm whose partners and customers always come back for more, are loyal, and help build business by word of mouth. In this scenario, both your tangible and intangible assets rise. This can create a unique niche for you in the market. Apple has consistently delivered to its customers, so they keep coming for more.

Unfortunately, trust is seen as an intangible versus a tangible by most, leading to the perception that building it, managing it, and leveraging it is a shot in the dark. However, according to Steven Covey in the *Speed of Trust*[54], this is far from the truth. Covey says that there are 13 behaviors of high-trust leaders, including showing loyalty, talking straight, creating transparency, and delivering results.

To manage the "how" of leveraging trust in business, there must be a sufficient framework to apply. Covey presents different spheres of trust as the "Five Waves of Trust". The first wave (Self-Trust) is to trust yourself. The second wave (Relationship Trust) is trust others.

The third through fifth waves represent "systems" of trust, including organizational, market, and societal. Covey refers to these "systems" of trust as Stakeholder Trust. Organizational Trust (the third wave) focuses on internal stakeholders while Market and Societal Trust (the fourth and fifth waves) focus on external stakeholders.

Covey's concept of Stakeholder Trust is on target, but it bypasses the dynamic, fluid, and complex nature of these systems. Covey's perspective does not adequately address inter-organizational/inter-market systems like joint ventures, alliances, partnerships, and value chains, which dominate the business environment today. Yet, trust is

---

[54] Covey, M.R. (2008). *The Speed of Trust: The One Thing that Changes Everything.* New York, NY: Free Press (Simon & Schuster).

the vital center for coordinating interaction in such systems, according to Bill McEvily, Vincenzo Perrone, and Akbar Zabeer.[55]

Another perspective, which accounts for the dynamic, fluid, and complex nature of stakeholder systems, is thinking of them as networks. A simple definition of a network is an interconnected system of things or people.

Networks are composed of nodes and their relationships. In people networks like markets, the nodes are people. The key questions for these networks are: 1) Who are the people? 2) How are they related? and 3) What do these relationships exchange and produce?

The concept of networks frames the business context in which trust plays a key role. Networks can frame organizations, industries, value chains, and markets. These are systems designed to create or increase value to its stakeholders. So when we speak of business or economic systems, we are speaking of "value" networks. "Value networks is any web of relationship that generates both intangible and tangible value through complex, dynamic exchanges between two or more individuals, groups, or organizations," according to Verna Allee of Value Networks.[56] This describes the networks that surround business and economic systems to a tee.

In actuality, trust and value brought by agents to an exchange both impact the exchange, but there aren't clear, precise boundaries for how these two elements interact, influence each other, and impact exchanges. For business, it's enough to know that trust can be leveraged for global business and that there are practical, simple ways to do so within the context of what I call "trust" networks.

---

[55] McEvily, B., Perrone, V., & Zabeer, A. (2003). Trust as an organizing principle. *Organization Science, 14*(1), 91-103.
[56] http://www.valuenetworks.com

A trust network is an overlay for a value network. The degree and type of trust that exists between people is one factor in determining what value they are willing to exchange and how they view and work in the relationship. So, as mentioned previously, trust has the central vital role for coordinating economic and value interactions and exchanges. Simply put, use trust to guide, organize, and manage your global business opportunities.

The concept of a trust network is not entirely new. On the web, in a similar fashion, trust networks exist. They are used so people can declare who they trust so others can see. There are other similar networks like reputation, which are normal for marketplaces and payment systems like Amazon, eBay, and PayPal. Users, who have more people who trust them or uphold their reputation, tend to draw business their way.

The power of trust networks is that anyone can put them to use for business. You don't need a certain amount of money, connections (a lot of people have connections that do not have high trust), information, and resources. As you work the methodology of trust networks, these things naturally come to as you build the right flows to achieve business success.

Steps for Building for a Trust Network for Global Business

One of the key misperceptions of going global is that you have to grow into it, developing enough capital resources to take on foreign markets. In reality, with the advent of telecommunications, the Internet, and technology, the cost of doing business globally can be a lot lower and within the budget and capacity of entrepreneurs and SMEs. Today, the resources that you can tap into, along with your own assets, shape your business opportunities. Hence, the importance of networks, particularly those built on trust, is evident because they allow you to tap into additional resources you do not have on your own.

Going global for an entrepreneur, or SME, can be costly, risky, and time consuming if done on his or her own. However, when you bring trusted associates into the equation, they can help spread the risk and reduce the time and cost to market.

Trust networks for global business start with the social and business networks an individual already has. An individual or organization works with "trusted" associates, configuring business strategy around the trust relationships and the information, resources, people, and capital they bring along with them.

The first step is to identify people within your formal, or informal, social and business networks to see who you trust. These are individual trust relationships. Openly talk about your business interests. It is often in these dialogues that opportunities appear.

The second step is to "chain" the individual trust relationships into a single, or a few, business opportunities. This results in a trust value chain to implement a business venture. If you choose the right trust relationships and opportunity frame, you can use this same chain over and over again to provide additional products and services to the same target market. The image on the following page illustrates a trust value chain.

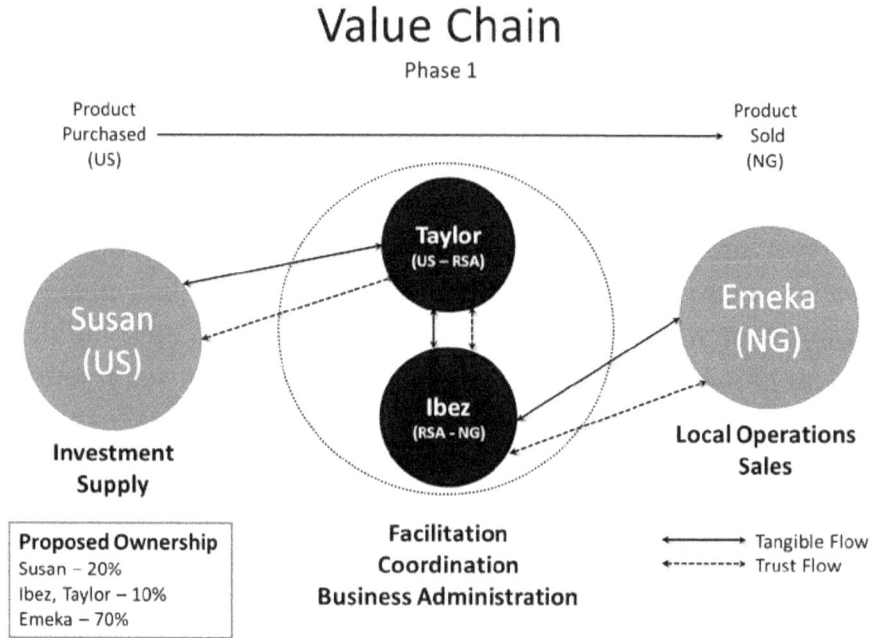

Value Chain
Phase 1

Product Purchased (US) ——————————————→ Product Sold (NG)

Taylor (US – RSA)

Susan (US)

Emeka (NG)

Ibez (RSA - NG)

Investment
Supply

Local Operations
Sales

Proposed Ownership
Susan – 20%
Ibez, Taylor – 10%
Emeka – 70%

**Facilitation
Coordination
Business Administration**

←——→ Tangible Flow
←------→ Trust Flow

Source: Lauri Elliott

In dealing with any global business opportunity, but in the context of Africa, it is recommended to work with people you trust locally. You cannot micromanage, nor should you, from a distance. So, trust value chains are one method for conducting business. This method allows quick and effective action with business opportunities.

For example, we recently identified a product in the United States that would be highly useful in Africa. Because we are familiar with the local markets, we have identified several sectors and consumers that would readily use the quality product. We didn't spend a lot of time in feasibility because we could enter the market for little cost and allow it to grow. However, to make it work, we identified a small investor and supplier from the U.S. to manage purchasing the product and someone locally in Africa to sell it. These were identified and established through individual relationships.

In another example, we used trust to improve the effectiveness of a project. In a recent experience, we re-configured a new venture by placing a point of contact between two key stakeholders that both of them trusted.

And the third step is to repeat steps 1 and 2 to establish a trust network, which multiplies the economic opportunities and growth for everyone involved. In the dynamics of networks, healthy networks will become alive and grow on their own. But you have to start with strategic intent, not a haphazard approach.

Trust is a Strategic Asset

As mentioned earlier, trust is also a strategic asset. It's important to view your trust network not only as a vehicle to do business globally, but more so as assets that can grow and increase in value themselves if managed well. Not doing so is probably the primary downfall of any trust network. Individuals in the network begin to take the people and relationships for granted and not putting in the proper care to make sure the network remains healthy.

It's important to realize what it means for someone to trust you. That person is willing to become vulnerable to you with the expectation that you will not harm him or her through intention or behavior. In business, that person or organization is expecting you to look out for his or her interest as well as your own.

The trust relationship established with someone is not the only sphere to consider when managing a trust network. You also need to acknowledge the impact and influence created on spheres within business, community, and society.

Individual trust relationships directly impact and influence organizations to which those in the trust relationship belong. For example, the information exchange between two people in different organizations, as a part of a joint venture, can help both organizations become more competitive in the market. On the other hand, a consultant (advising a technology company), who learns the details of a new technology roll-out, and shares these details with outsiders so they can buy or sell stock in anticipation of this move, violates the trust the technology company placed in the consultant.

This last example has broader implications because it gives the stock traders unfair advantage over others, who might choose to buy or sell the stock. And, this type of breach of trust is actually against the law. The consultant has bankrupted his trust asset base just in this one act.

So, as you manage your portfolio of assets to grow wealth, you do the same with trust assets.

Building Trust in Individual Relationships

Since individuals are the lowest common denominator in a trust network, they should be seen as the essential building blocks for a trust network. As an individual, you need to consider both how you trust yourself and how you trust others. Healthy high-trust relationships can only be developed when individuals are able to trust themselves and willing to trust others. When considering your position in trust relationships, you should ask and address the following questions:

- Do you trust yourself to operate with integrity?
- Do you trust yourself to bear good intentions to others who trust you?
- Do you trust that you have the capacity to carry out what is asked of you? Within which boundaries, do you trust your capacity?
- Do you trust yourself to get results?
- Are you more prone to trust or distrust others?

Individuals inherently trust themselves and others in some instances and distrust in other instances. A few ways to engender trust within yourself:

- Learn to operate within the strengths and value you bring. Keep from being drawn into situations where you know you can't deliver.
- Only promise what you feel comfortable delivering.
- Deliver more than you promise.
- Don't be too critical of yourself. Be willing to forgive your own faults.

To engender trust within individual trust relationships, do the following:

- Listen more and when you do speak, speak plainly and straightforward.
- Show respect and deference for others.
- Be transparent as appropriate.
- Make yourself accountable to others and hold others accountable.
- Clarify expectations and keep commitments.
- Work on making relationships better.
- Be loyal.
- Correct mistakes or wrongdoings.
- Be alert for conflicts of interest and make others aware when they exist.
- Become vulnerable to the other person in the trust relationship.
- Share or give something to the other person in the trust relationship that they would value without asking for anything back.
- Keep someone's secrets whether or not they ask you to.

- If you make a mistake, whether you are caught or not, confess at the appropriate time and venue and ask for forgiveness.
- Be willing to lay down your interests for the interests of others when called for.

Applying Trust in Business Scenarios

In business, people tend to mostly think of the value others bring when entering agreements. That is the first decision point, but the second decision point, and often the final decision point, should be do you trust the person?

If you have any qualms on trusting the person at any level, you need to configure the agreement so that you are comfortable with the level of trust you are placing in the person. For example, a person has performed well for others previously, but your project has a much larger scale. If possible, split the project between two persons if you cannot find one person with which you feel comfortable.

And there are other times, when you have to stretch your "trust" muscles to take advantage of opportunities. Find ways to minimize risks within these trust relationships. For example, configure project or venture so that breach of trust brings big negative consequences. If a person is looking to grow his or her business within a certain network or market in which you have a lot of influence, shape agreement so the individual understands the power your relationship brings and the loss he or she would experience if things didn't work out.

If you cannot establish a level of trust that will work for the project or venture, think about walking away for the time being. Often, people who enter agreements in these instances look for problems and micromanage others, which puts undue stress on the relationship and adds intangible and tangible costs to the project.

When considering entering, the current state of, or future of a trust relationship, ask yourself the following questions:

- How well will (or do) you demonstrate trustworthy behaviors?
- How well will (or does) the other person demonstrate trustworthy behaviors in this situation?
- What is the state of the relationship? Is it new, developing, or long sustained? Is it healthy or dysfunctional?
- Do you implicitly trust the person? With what things do you trust the person? With what things do you not trust the person?
- What do you like about the person and what can you rely on from that person?
- Is there any behavior that has to be confronted? If so, how are you going to handle it?
- What impact will trusting or not trusting a person have on the project or venture?
- What things can you do to build trust fast and strong?
- Are you focusing on costs or value creation? Conversations about value creation enable trust.
- What remedies do you have if things go wrong?

There are also different scenarios, e.g., new versus long-standing relationships, for applying trust in projects or ventures. Here are a few practical tips for projects around trust:

- Differentiate between projects that require working with people who need to earn your trust (on critical components) and those working with people who have already earned your trust.
- For projects/ventures working with people earning your trust, establish a manageable scope for six months to one year so that you can explore opportunities and relationships.

- Place critical components of a trust value chain, or a project, only in hands of people you implicitly trust.
- Develop a trust value chain from a core group of three to 12 people (a group that will hold each other accountable).
- Each group member, identify three people in business or professions they implicitly trust that fit the project/venture.
- Scope project/venture based on capacity within trust boundaries (for critical components).

You also need to assess the health of each key individual trust relationship periodically. In doing so, you need to decide if it needs maintaining, pruning, or cutting and take appropriate action.

Considerations for Value Network Versus Trust Network

Focusing on individual trust relationships helps you discover the quality of the relationships within your network, which will help leverage available assets and resources. However, it's important to understand exactly what exchanges, flows, and deliverables occur within your network so you know what you can leverage.

While not covered here, it is easy enough to frame your network in terms of value by asking the following questions:

- Who are the people (or roles) in the network?
- What deliverables, exchanges, and flows occur in the network?
- Who is involved with each deliverable, exchange, and flow in the network?
- How well do the deliverables, exchanges, and flows occur with the people involved?
- From the previous elements, what value lies in the network?
- How can you improve and leverage the value in the network?

The best of all worlds is where you have a network filled with high-trust and high-value. Choices of whom to work with should be a combination of trust and the value each person brings. However, this is not a typical scenario unless you have been working on it with intent.

If you have a situation where someone brings high-value, but adequate trust is not present, see if you can discover a scope that allows for adequate trust and still takes advantage of the high-value the person brings. If you trust the person, but they do not bring sufficient value to the project, see if you can discover a scope that will bring forth the value and take advantage of the trust.

In either situation, if you cannot find an equation that brings both sufficient trust and value, I recommend that you walk away for the time being.

People and the Trust Network

This piece focused on how to leverage trust to transform global business opportunities. As with any methodology though, it can become mechanistic when focus is placed on the tasks and activities of managing trust rather than the people involved.

What was presented here should be used as a guideline and framework for facilitating trust relationships so you can see improved business performance. However, if you lose your connection to the people in the process, you defeat your initial purpose and the power of the trust network.

To keep yourself grounded, ask yourself the following questions:

- Do I care about the relationships and people within the network?
- Am I serving and looking out for the interests of the people in the network, even if it means sacrifices on my part?
- Is what I'm doing helping or harming people?
- What will I lose if I lose the trust of these people?
- Is what I am doing worth losing the trust?

Remember, the common denominator in any organization, community, society, market, or industry is the people involved. People are the reason that these spheres exist and people are the reason we are able to create wealth. If we harm or abuse them, it can at some point impact profitability.

There is something I was reminded of recently, and something none of us should ever forget, God often asks us to do things that we would not naturally do and do not understand, including entering covenants that may seem to have very little value for us at the time. While I stressed the importance of configuring high-value, high-trust scenarios, it is more important to follow the leading of the Lord. And ultimately, we are to put our trust in God not man.

Conclusion

Most consider trust an intangible asset, if an asset at all. But while it may not take physical form as currency, it is tangible in the behaviors exhibited by people in relationships.

High-trust relationships provide many benefits for businesses, including faster execution, lower costs, and even improved competitive advantage. These relationships situated in networks of business interests direct where flows of capital, information, resources, and assets go.

Trust networks employ the methodology of using trust, along with value, to configure business strategy for global business. Trust networks are developed in steps – from trust relationships, to trust value chains, to trust networks.

Individuals are the lowest common denominator in trust networks, so how individuals trust themselves and others and how well those relationships develop mutual trust, impact the health of the entire network.

Using a trust network to strategically leverage business opportunities is the macro level, but the trust network itself must be facilitated first and primarily through the micro level which are the relationships themselves. For Christians, this includes our vertical relationship with God.

8

Closing:
Challenges and Navigating the Path
Nissi Ekpott
Lauri Elliott

Even with all the positive paradigms shared about Africa in this book, there are still realities that need to be faced in Africa and ways to navigate your starting path that need to be shared. In this closing, we cover both.

Challenges
Africa presents one of the world's last big opportunities and in this book we have offered pointers towards these opportunities. However, doing business in Africa is not a bed of roses; on the contrary, investors need to be prepared for the challenges they may face.

Just like the European pioneers, who explored North America, faced and overcame its overwhelming challenges, those wanting to do business in Africa, at this phase of its development, need to see themselves as explorers, adventurers, and advancers in a new and fast emerging frontier. There are many challenges, and it would be impossible to discuss them all in this book, but here are a few to look out for.

Governance
Governance is improving. However, it is still far from ideal in many parts of the continent.

Conflict and Strife

From a peak of over 15 active wars in 1999, wars on the continent have reduced to less than five. However, there are still fragile areas within post-conflict nations, border areas, etc. There are pockets of local conflicts still happening.

It is necessary to carry out proper research about these areas, and avoid them, if possible. If working or doing business there is an absolute necessity, then seek practical advice on how to navigate and to reduce risk.

Security

Africa can be a dangerous place depending on where you are. Most countries are still in a recovery state, and though security is slowly improving, investors and visitors to the continent still need to approach these countries with care. Nigeria, Liberia, Sierra Leone and Kenya are showing improvements in their state of security. Rwanda has shown very rapid improvement and its capital, Kigali, is arguably one of Africa's safest cities.

Visiting and living in some parts of Africa may require that you change your lifestyle to adapt to local conditions. For instance, you may not be able to take walks on the streets, you may have to live behind high walls, and you may need security guards at entrance gates.

But not to worry, there are very practical ways to adapt. There are secure parks where you can walk, bike, walk your dog, or relax. In some places, such as South Africa, there are gated communities where you can find as much activity as you would require anywhere else. It is necessary for visitors to Africa to seek counsel and reside in safer areas.

Can't Trust Everyone

We've talked a lot about trust. However, it shouldn't be done blindly. Make wise choices.

If you are doing business in Africa, like everywhere else globally, do not trust people blindly. There are people who are simply out there to defraud. Do not take on a local business partner in a trusting and naive way. Make efforts to verify the credibility of the people you work with.

Can't Believe Everything You Hear

Do not believe all you hear especially from governments and state-run media, which is very rampant in Africa. Always try to hear the other side of the story from the ordinary people. Do sufficient independent research and then make informed decisions.

Bureaucracy

Africa is far more bureaucratic than your wildest imaginations. Licenses and registrations are needed for almost everything and it sometimes takes very long to achieve them. Some of these delays are just pure inefficiency, while others are deliberate opportunities for corruption.

Some African nations, such as Rwanda and Ghana, have been among global top reformers in improving their business processes, while others remain far behind. You need to find ways to absorb these delays into your overall project plan.

There are usually local agencies, such as business consultants, finance houses, and legal firms, who offer services to help foreign nationals process the myriad of local requirements. Sometimes it is advisable to use their services. They may seem expensive, but you will find out that they save you lots of time and actually work out cheaper in the long run than if you tried to do it yourself.

Corruption

Corruption remains a major challenge in most of Africa. The corruption is sometimes systemic and is not always recognized for what it is. But, bear in mind that there are many Africans who do not buy into corruption, and there will always be a way to navigate and avoid it.

UAC, a Nigerian company set up by the British over a hundred years ago, publicly declares that in its years of doing business in Nigeria it has never paid a bribe. Steve Shelley, author of *Doing Business in Africa*[57], a British indigene who has lived and done business in at least twenty African countries over the past 25 years, states in his book that he has never had to be involved in corrupt practices.

Culture

Africa is not your country; there will be many differences in language, culture, and so on. Even if you speak the same language as the country you visit and in which you do business, look out for the fact that the meanings may be different.

Most African English-speaking countries, for instance, South Africa, Nigeria, and Kenya, have their own variety of English, and there are sometimes distinct differences. Cultures also differ from country to country, and in many cases some countries have differing cultures within them.

Nigeria, for instance, has over three hundred different ethnic groups, some with very distinct differences. Tanzania has over a hundred different ethnic groups, while South Africa has at least eleven.

---

[57] Shelley, S. (2004). *Doing Business in Africa: A Practical Guide for Investors, Entrepreneurs and Expatriate Managers*. New York, NY: Zebra Books.

In my (Nissi's) discussions with people who have visited Africa and decided to stay and do business, the one area that seems to be the biggest challenge has been cultural differences. Culture can make or break everything.

You need to be prepared for the differences in culture. Bear in mind that living in a place is different from visiting for a couple of weeks or months. This applies globally and Africa is no different.

Western visitors to South Africa are first amazed at the similarities to their nations in terms of look and feel, and then are shocked at the differences in terms of people and culture. Some things will be familiar to you, but many things different, and within individual countries there are many cultural differences. Some key cultural issues to watch out for:

- **Punctuality and time**: In most African cultures, time is like a flowing river, it is not exact, and there is no pressure to catch it because you can always get another part of it. Time based appointments are not expected to be kept. It sometimes applies differently to social functions than to official functions. In parts of West Africa, it is actually against the norm to arrive for a wedding on time, and more acceptable to be there two hours late. For official meetings, it varies and generally, thirty minutes to one hour late may be acceptable. In dealing with government officials, you will find in some places that they may not turn up for the entire day, regardless of the appointments in their schedule. The increased usage of mobile phones has served to help; you can find out where the person you are meeting is, and decide if the scheduled time is realistic. Always try to get their phone numbers and call ahead, and always have another potential activity you could do with your time if a meeting is rescheduled or canceled. On the other hand, there are countries like Botswana where it is considered impolite when you come five minutes late.

- **Slow down**: Things do not move as fast in Africa.
- **Taking calls during meetings**: In some parts of Africa, such as South Africa, this is considered rude and generally not accepted except with the permission of the other people. However, in other countries, such as Nigeria, taking calls during meetings is acceptable.
- **Courtesy and social manners**: This occupies a place of high importance in most African cultures. Social greetings and exchanges are required, and you could lose a lot of respect for ignoring this. Handshakes, hugs, greetings, and small talk about the spouse and the family are part of the culture. These usually precede most conversations, including business.
- **Family**: African societies place high importance on family. People work from the basis of family. Because most African countries have an inefficient citizen tracking system, people rely on family relationships to establish credibility. Families are also very useful for arbitration and conflict resolution. There is usually a thin line between working through family networks and nepotism, but if you have to succeed in Africa, you need to come to terms that the culture works this way. People relate with each other beyond the individuals and reach out to their families.
- **Dress code**: In most parts of Sub-Saharan Africa, formal dressing is required for formal occasions, such as business meetings, church events, and so on. This is regardless of the hot climate. Some parts are sensitive to women's and men's clothing. Women visiting Africa should take care to ask about the dress codes.

- **Entertaining and social events**: Most African cultures are very much into entertaining and social functions, everything calls for a celebration – a marriage, birthday, burial, and festive seasons - and it is usually a large celebration. Huge crowds turn up for seemingly unimportant events. And you will be expected to attend. So, sharpen your social skills!

- **Language**: Most people in Africa speak at least two languages – one of the main languages, i.e., English or French, and a local language. These main languages are usually the common language within a nation and help them overcome the wide ethnic and language diversity. However, keep in mind that it is usually not their first language and hence may be expressed in a way different to what you understand. Always try to clarify things, and keep discussions simple.

- **Business expenses**: These can be very high in many parts of Africa. Sometimes where there is no consistent electricity, you need to factor in the cost of a backup generator and the fuel to run it. In some cities, such as Lagos, you may find it easier to get yourself a chauffeur. This is an added cost. Salaries are low, but sometimes this advantage is stolen by low productivity. Investors should place a premium on employee training and improving work ethics and productivity. Manufactured items are mostly imported, so they are more expensive in many parts of the continent, these include things like vehicles, electronic equipment, phones, etc.

- **Diseases**: Malaria, HIV/AIDS, and several other diseases are rampant in Africa. The high prevalence of these diseases affects worker productivity, and in many parts of the continent, citizens do not have health insurance services, so investors need to factor this in while planning. Foreign visitors should ensure they have necessary vaccinations.

- **Poor infrastructure especially in West and Central Africa:** The roads can be very bad and in many cases non-existent. As much as possible, travel should be done by air. Where road travel is unavoidable, make provision for the delays. Where you can, avoid on-land, cross border travel as these places can be quite corrupt at times. Electricity supply can be epileptic in some parts, so if you have to set up private residence, you need to think of standby power. Since the water infrastructure is poor in some places and non-existent in others, you may need to consider buying bottled water, or drilling a borehole.

These are just a summary of things to look at. In the book, *Doing Business in Africa* by Steve Shelley, you will find a lot more detail on the day-to-day issues you may face, and recommendations on how to tackle these. Remember, Africa consists of 53 countries (soon to be 54 countries with the addition of Southern Sudan), and these challenges are not necessarily found in all the countries. Some parts of Africa can favorably match western standards in varying ways.

Navigating the Path

This book has established that God has hidden, or allowed to be obscured, the wealth potential of Africa to broadly benefit His people and through them the nations. Because of the extent of the Christian Church throughout Africa, particularly Sub-Saharan Africa, Christians have a competitive advantage to do business and investment there. Yet for the most part, we are allowing our opportunities to waste away.

And while we (Hartmut, Nissi, and Lauri) know the blessing of doing business in Africa, we recognize and share challenges you will face. Life is a journey, so is Africa. God has designed us to face and solve challenges. If you are ready to start this journey we have a little more to share with you.

So, how do you get started with tapping into the opportunities in Africa? We have pointed out the methodology for shaping your business strategy around opportunities presented through your trust networks. This is the anchor, but there is a process to carry out which is the focus of this section.

First, I (Lauri) want to mention that not everyone will want to venture into business themselves, but will be willing to invest. In fact, investing is often a preferred method for people since they do not need to become an expert but can rely on those who are to create successful ventures and partnering with them to do so.

If you are into stocks, you can look at how to diversify your portfolio to include firms that operate in Africa. There are several mechanisms for tapping publicly listed companies on over 20 stock exchanges in Africa. You can learn more in Hartmut's primer, *Tapping the Wealth of African Stocks: Building a Valuable Stock Portfolio.*[58]

You can also invest in private ventures directly or indirectly. There are venture projects for which people are looking for investors. At another level, you can invest in a private equity fund, which is managed by a fund manager and consists of several or many projects. You can contact Hartmut (www.trans-africa-invest.com) to learn more.

---

[58] Learn more at http://www.afribiz.net/content/starting-a-stock-portfolio-for-africa-a-book.

Some of you have ideas for products and services that you want to export to the African markets or import from African markets to the U.S. and other global regions. Nissi (www.neuafrika.com) has terrific insights into the African markets and can assist with importing and exporting products, as well as establishing a business there.

One key recommendation beyond working with people that you trust is that whether you invest or decide to do business in Africa, don't go it alone. If you are going to invest, think about forming an investment club with several people to share the experience and spread the risk. If you are going to form a business, find strategic business partners on your side of the world not just local partners in Africa. While it can sometimes be challenging to work with a group, your collective learning, insights, and perspectives can create substantial intangible assets as you develop more projects.

If you decide to do a business venture in Africa and you have little or no experience, here are a series of steps to help you walk through from start to completing your first year in operation. The time frame is from 15 to 18 months. This process is also designed for proof-of-concept or pilot business ventures to flush out the detail in a business venture. For a larger project, you can consult directly with Hartmut, Nissi, or me.

The first six months focus on identifying, shaping, planning, and launching the business venture. The following steps, which come from my audio, book, and coaching series, *Going Global on a Dime* (www.goingglobalonadime.com), are generally completed in this order, but can be iterative in nature:

1. Identify your strengths, or capital assets, which may be both tangible and intangible.
2. Conduct initial research to learn more about opportunities, sources, countries, markets, and global issues that will help

shape your strategy. Research is a continual process throughout this three- to six-month period.

3.   Learn about issues that impact your business globally and in a particular country, e.g., regulations, labor laws, countries and products which are banned by your government, intellectual property.

4.   Develop your company and product brand. Once you define your brand, you also need to produce a profile, brochure, website, business cards, and other appropriate marketing materials.

5.   Go out (both online and offline) to explore your networks to identify people and organizations with which you can potentially work. Build your ecosystem to support the value chain you will have to develop to carry out the venture.

6.   Prioritize opportunities based on your strengths, including your ecosystem. Continue with high priority opportunities.

7.   Draft an initial business model for each of the high priority opportunities. You only want to work on 1-3 opportunities at a time.

8.   Use the business models as discussion documents to draw partners and resources. Resist the urge to approach investors until you have a concrete plan.

9.   After your discussions and after you have chosen the one opportunity to pursue, flush out customer profile, as well as supply chain and marketing channels to customer.

10. Flush out revenue and operational model, as well as cost structure.

11. Develop a concept document, which will be used to frame your business venture.

12. Sign non-disclosure/non-compete agreements with partners, investors, providers, etc.

13. Develop initial project plan, budget, and cash flow projections for the first year of the venture.
14. Shape your business strategy to work within the scope and parameters that will leverage your assets, keep costs low, have potentially significant outcomes that can be scaled, and will accelerate cash flow.
15. Sign joint venture agreement (based on outlined business strategy) and finalize project plan and budget.
16. Implement and operate first-year plan.[59]
17. Monitor progress and adapt as necessary.
18. Conduct quarterly reviews of business.
19. Conduct a review of the first year.
20. Determine next phase of business operation.

During this initial stage, it is important to leverage assets that you have and minimize risk, some pointers include:

- Look for low-hanging fruit and opportunities.
- Do sufficient due diligence as befits the size of investment.
- Choose small, but significant opportunities that can be scaled.
- Resist the urge to go into debt in early-stage ventures.
- Include people that you have strong trust relationships as part of your core team.
- Don't promise or expect too much from partners.
- Be honest and open to promote transparency, but be wise in what, how, to whom, and when you share.
- Conduct regular status meetings and prepare reports. (Some Africans do not prefer to write, so you can do an oral report and take good notes.)
- Expect change and be willing to adapt.
- And, most of all follow the leading of the Holy Spirit.

---

[59] For a sample plan, send an email to info@conceptualee.com.

Conclusion

You will find investing in Africa a profitable learning curve. You will encounter a spirit of enterprise like you have never experienced, all across the continent. You will see unbridled hope, optimism, laughter, celebration, and zeal in the midst of many challenges. You will see and experience a level of spirituality, trust, and dependence on God that is mind blowing.

Investing, living, or working among Africans will change your life, not only financially, but in every other way, too.

Above all these, as children of God, we should always seek Godly counsel in all we do. Not all that looks good is actually good, and not all that looks bad, is really bad. Sometimes great gifts come in ugly packages.

The story is told that the first diamonds to be discovered in Kimberly, South Africa, were found by kids who thought it was just a bright stone and kicked it around and played with it. The diamond eventually found its way into the right hands, and the rest is history – the economy of that nation changed forever. A lot of Africa is like a diamond in the rough, but God promises to lead and guide his people in the way they should go. This should undergird our approach to business in Africa.

Also, you will never find the perfect time for venturing out into Africa, so it's important to have the frame of mind to be committed to doing it if you are directed and in the Lord's time. Any path of promise has its giants like the children of Israel encountered as they took possession of the land. So, expect challenges, but also expect victory through Christ.

And finally, Africa is a "big" place with so much to offer. It's like getting a big dose of oxygen into your system. So, as you experience it and its people, let your spirit be enlivened.

We wish you the greatest blessings on your journey as you follow the Lord.

Appendix A:
African New Economy Workgroup (ANEW)

Hartmut, Nissi, and Lauri are the lead facilitators for the African New Economy Workgroup (ANEW). The purpose of ANEW is to catalyze and accelerate economic opportunity and development in Africa and the diaspora that is open, inclusive, and benefits all by approaching our social/informal/business networks and global value chains as a single economy.

While God is the source of all and the Christian community our brotherhood, ANEW is an open organism welcoming all who can "connect" with its vision and abide by its ethical framework to release the tapped wealth in Africa to its people and through its people bring wealth to the world.

How Does ANEW Describe an Economy?

An economy is a system of production, exchange, distribution, and consumption of goods and services. It is a system of creating, increasing, and transforming value.

However, ANEW sees an economy as both a platform for exchange and community. In fact, ANEW's economy is constructed based on people and their relationships. It takes a human ecological view of economy in which people are the foci and all other elements support the prosperity of people. Therefore, institutions, processes, procedures, etc., serve people not the other way around.

In essence, ANEW's economy is a social network transformed to a value network – a network that has a purpose. In this case, the purpose is to promote economic prosperity along the African trade routes. The economy is held together by the trust that exists between the people in ANEW.

The economic system assures that economic justice, opportunity, and prosperity is spread to active "citizens" of ANEW.

The economy takes on a unique configuration of elements from virtual, geographic, and alternative economies. Its scope is expansive, but aligns with its objectives. It is not defined by a rigid framework.

The nature of the economy is self-sustaining, growing/expanding, and able to handle the turbulent, fast, and chaotic environment of today. It does this by maintaining an organic, fluid state, which is achieved by agility.

The ANEW economy will be a model for what we call a "conduit" economy.

What is ANEW's Key Message?

Exploring, embracing, engaging, and expanding to alternative markets in and through Africa to create exponential opportunities for growing sustainable business and fostering and maximizing benefits to all key stakeholders.

The future of our world is multi-polar, meaning that one or a few countries will no longer hold the economic or political power over the entire world. Instead, each country will have its own unique space and strengths in all spheres, including economic, political, and cultural. Our world will move fluidly and dynamically, where possible, like living systems interconnected.

In terms of the global economy, this means creating multi-growth poles - stimulating and catalyzing growth in every region and leveraging for global growth instead of relying on growth in one or a few countries like the United States in the past to fuel growth. There will, of course, be countries that will represent larger growth opportunities at different stages based on different variables like size of population. Good examples are China and India.

Every perspective, or every growth region, will provide opportunities in their local, regional, and global markets. This holds true for Africa and Africa is already positioned to serve as one pole, an epicenter, and an open gateway to trade, investment, and business to emerging markets like Brazil, China, India, and Russia, and even to the developed world.

The key phrase in our message is "alternative" markets. What we mean by "alternative" markets are markets in addition to your existing market not necessarily instead of. This approach is based on the principle of alternative, multiple, or diversified streams of revenue. If we think of economies, more diversified economies typically can withstand external shocks better and this is what you want to do for your enterprise so you can continue to grow and generate profit.

When we speak of markets, it could refer to places like Nigeria, China, Vietnam, and Argentina. But markets also mean different things, e.g., industries, online, microniches, and metamarkets. When you think about the word "market," think outside of the normal definition for markets. This will help you see more opportunities.

When we talk about opportunities, there is a simple principle called adjacent opportunities. Adjacent opportunities, coined by Ronald Schultz, are those that are only a step away and came into existence because of previous actions. So, if you never go through the process of exploring, embracing, engaging, and expanding in and through Africa, you will not likely discover nor apprehend the exponential opportunities for growing sustainable businesses available by connecting with Africa.

When you explore, it means taking a look at potential opportunities by doing initial research, talking with people, etc. When you embrace, it means deciding that you will pursue Africa as a channel to create exponential growth opportunities for your business. When you engage, it means acting on that decision. And, when you expand, it means finally implementing one, several, or many of the opportunities. These activities are part of an iterative process called E^4.

And finally, notice that we say "in and through" Africa. Africa is not only positioned to be a pole of growth in itself, but as a conduit for global business and trade. Africa has become an epicenter and open gateway for international trade. This has quietly snuck up on the world.

What is ANEW Doing Now?

2011 is the year in which ANEW will initiate its "conduit" economy with specific projects. These projects include gold mining, agriculture, ICT, media and broadcasting, and importing and exporting channels. The projects will be in and through Africa and to emerging markets like Brazil, India, and China, as well as to the United States, Germany, and other developed countries. For more information, send an email to anew@conceptualee.com.

Lauri Elliott

God has chosen Lauri to be a vessel to share the strength in business, media, and education that she is divinely given (Isaiah 32:2). This is manifested in Lauri's role as a strategist with over 25 years of business experience, specializing in global business, innovation, technology, and new ventures and start-ups. She serves entrepreneurs, small, micro, and medium-size enterprises (SMMEs), and individual investors.

As the Director of Afribiz™ Media, a Division of Conceptualee, Inc., Lauri has developed a solid reputation as a new media leader. She is the primary host of Afribiz.fm™, a regular online radio show about doing business and investing in Africa. She also writes frequently for publications such as *Brainstorm* magazine, an ITWeb publication, in South Africa.

In addition, Lauri is the author of *Export to Explode Cash Flow and Profits: Creating New Streams of Business in Asia, Africa, and the Americas* and *Going Global on a Dime: The Entrepreneur's Handbook to Tapping the Global Marketplace.*

Lauri operates out of the apostolic, prophetic, and teaching ministries. To reach Lauri, visit http://www.lauri-elliott.com.

Nissi Ekpott

Nissi is a Christian entrepreneur, business developer, and catalyst for African restoration. Raised in Nigeria, he started his first business – a dry cleaning service - at the age of 15. Over the years, he gained experience through conventional education, and several hands-on experiences.

Nissi consults for small and big businesses in Africa, touching business and leadership development and providing services, including business tours and training programs for public and private sector officials.

Nissi coordinates BizConnect Afrika, a place businesses connect, as well as share ideas, opportunities, and resources. He also serves as a business journalist for Afribiz.net, a media brand of Conceptualee, Inc. (U.S.) and other websites and magazines in South Africa.

Nissi believes in the Word of God, and its power to transform people, nations, and systems. He functions in a prophetic ministry, with a God-given understanding of biblical worldview.

He lives in Johannesburg, South Africa with his wife and two beautiful daughters. To reach Nissi, visit http://www.neuafrika.com.

Hartmut Sieper

Hartmut is a Christian banker, business consultant, and investment specialist.

Hartmut is convinced that the time has come for Africa to arise in many aspects, including business and finance. In anticipating this trend and by following God's guidance, he has founded the company Trans Africa Invest to attract businesses, companies, and investors from German-speaking countries to African markets. He is working closely together with local partners in 15 African countries. He is the sole investment adviser of a Luxembourg-based, Pan-African mutual fund which is investing in listed African securities.

He has written several books about investing. His latest books are *Investing in Africa – The Wealth of the Black Continent* and *Cape of Good Business – Strategies for Long-Term Success in South Africa* (both are written in German), as well as *Tapping the Wealth of African Stocks*. In the German media, he is considered as one of the leading Africa experts in Germany.

Hartmut is married and lives in northern Bavaria, Germany. He attends a free evangelical local church. Since 2006, he is a member of the International Christian Chamber of Commerce, ICCC. Hartmut can be reached at http://www.trans-africa-invest.com.

BizConnect Africa

www.bizconnectafrika.biz

*You want to get into Africa and do business,
but you do not know anyone in Africa.*

- How do you find credible networks and connect to real business people?
- How do you find "on the ground" information?
- How do you test your ideas and share ideas and resources?
- How do you gain a relational entry point into the continent?

BizConnect Afrika is a business network established to share ideas, opportunities, and resources between its members. BizConnect Afrika is designed to encourage the building of relationships and community through business. It is a virtual/face-to-face business network that bridges and connects businesses beyond borders.

BizConnect Afrika members realize that even though business is good, business deals are temporal while relationships are eternal. Hence, relationship and community building is necessary for true success.

Visit the BizConnect Afrika website at *www.bizconnectafrika.biz*. Register online and become part of a business community with a focus on Africa.

Trans Africa Invest

www.trans-africa-invest.com

You want to invest in Africa, but you do not know how.

- How do you find investment projects in specific sectors and countries where you can invest?
- How do you find reliable investment managers with strong local expertise in Africa, who are following Kingdom-based principles that are described in this book?
- How do you reduce investment risk?

Trans Africa Invest is a Germany-based investment and consultancy firm that introduces investors, companies, and technologies from developed countries into African growth markets.

Through private equity (PE) funds, which are launching in 2011, investors can choose viable projects in various African countries and different economic sectors in which to invest. An international team of investment professionals, both from Africa and the developed world, will manage the PE funds and support the portfolio companies in doing their businesses, thereby adding value to the portfolios. The PE funds will be domiciled in a well-known financial center, i.e. Mauritius. In 2011, we are specifically looking for:

- Viable projects in Africa (business plan is required)
- Investors that want to have exposure in Africa in a broad range of attractive projects in various countries
- Financial intermediaries in U.S. and selected European countries that will connect domestic investors with African investment projects, either by participating in our private equity funds or by creating joint ventures

Afribiz

www.afribiz.info

*You want to learn more about business in Africa,
but you don't know where to go.*

*Afribiz.info is the leading, and premier, independent portal about
doing business and investing in Africa.*

Afribiz provides free and premium resources, intelligence, information, tools, insights, and strategies to help you navigate business and investment in Africa. If you want to know something about business in Africa, Afribiz is the best place to start.

Afribiz.info is our portal bringing together resources about African business from around the world into one place. No need to find resources one by one. We help you accelerate your research and strategy efforts.

Afribiz.net is the site for our premium, mostly original content provided as text, audio, and video that can be interacted with across computing and mobile platforms.

Afribiz.fm (www.blogtalkradio.com/afribiz) is our publicly broadcast audio content. Hear from experts and entrepreneurs how they make things happen in business in Africa. This is no ordinary program. You hear and learn what you can do to make things happen for you.

We also develop publications, e.g., books, magazines, and guides, conduct webinars and teleconferences (live and on-demand), host face-to-face events, and provide facilitation and consulting to help you navigate business in Africa successfully.

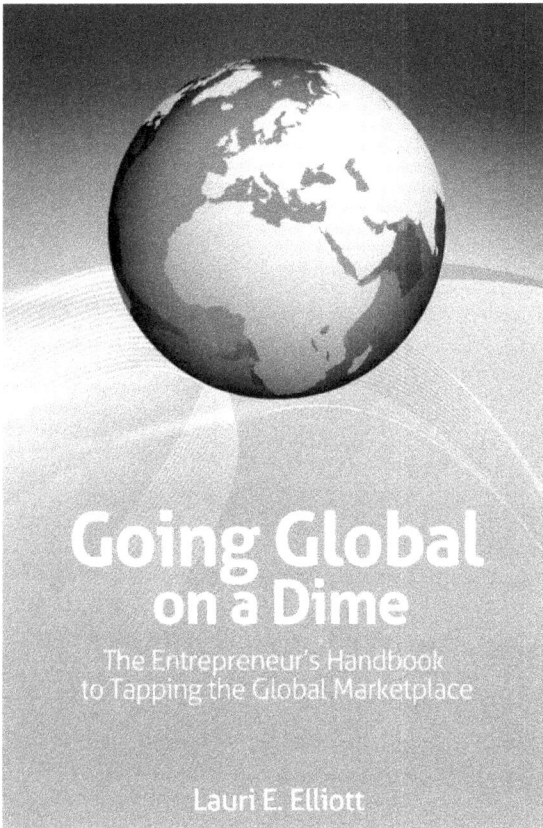

Going Global
on a Dime
The Entrepreneur's Handbook
to Tapping the Global Marketplace

Lauri E. Elliott

www.goingglobalonadime.com

Going Global on a Dime answers the "how" of going global from both a strategic and practical approach, focusing on new and existing firms considering or just starting the going global process. It re-wires the framework for going global so firms can navigate the course dynamically while minimizing costs, managing and maximizing cash flow and return on investment, streamlining processes, and keeping the "small" firm ready to take advantage of profitable opportunities.

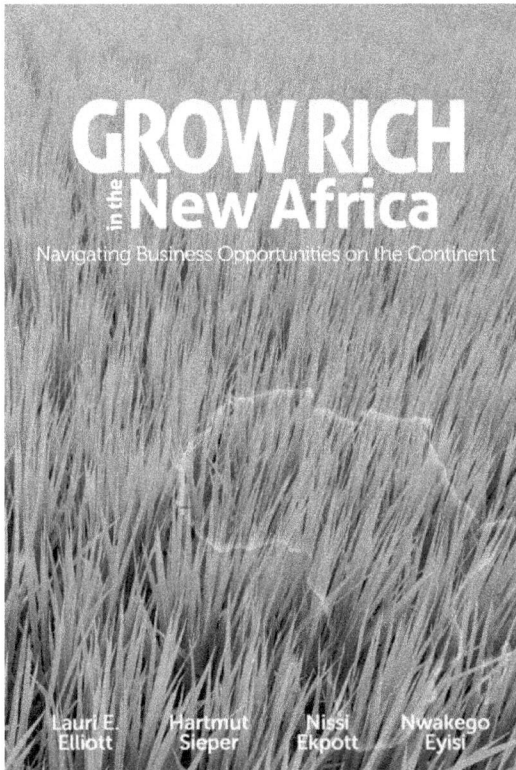

www.grow-rich-in-the-new-africa.com

Africa is the place to be for the next generation of business opportunities. As a follow-up to *Creating Wealth by Harnessing Opportunities in Africa*, this book delves more into how to do business in Africa. You will learn:

- Major sector, e.g., ICT, real estate, opportunities going into the future
- Consumer markets in Africa
- Strategies to consider for doing business in Africa
- How to leverage your existing resources to do business in Africa.

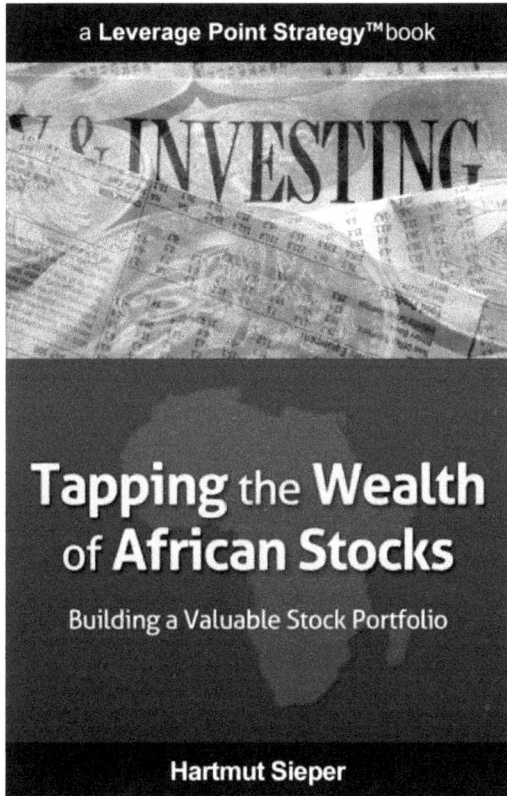

a Leverage Point Strategy™ book

INVESTING

Tapping the Wealth of African Stocks

Building a Valuable Stock Portfolio

Hartmut Sieper

www.tapping-wealth-of-african-stocks.com

Warren Buffet says, "The critical investment factor is determining the intrinsic value of a business and paying a fair or bargain price." Where can investors go to find these businesses today?

Africa is one place. "African stocks continue to be undervalued, providing greater value for investors interested in long-term investments," says Hartmut Sieper, the author. *Tapping the Wealth of African Stocks* focuses on helping individual investors understand how to access African stock markets.

a **Leverage Point Strategy**™ book

Export
to
EXPLODE
Cash Flow and Profits

Creating New Streams of Business in
Asia, Africa, and the Americas
with Little Investment

Lauri E. Elliott

www.export-to-explode-cash-flow.com

Exporting is one of the strategies for conducting international business or trade. With the *squeeze* on businesses during the global economic recovery, there is no better time to explore new avenues to generate revenues and profits. *Export to Explode Cash Flow and Profits* specifically shares 12 different leverage points, e.g., demand-driven exporting, multinational ecosystems, and cities and economic hubs that you can use to help formulate strategies for exporting to the emerging markets in Asia, Africa, and the Americas.

www.ingramcontent.com/pod-product-compliance
Lightning Source LLC
Chambersburg PA
CBHW031325210326
41519CB00048B/3140